a guide to prayer

Opening To God

a guide to prayer

Opening To God

Thomas H. Green, S.J.

Ave Maria Press
Notre Dame, Indiana 46556

Imprimi potest:
 Joaquin G. Bernas, S.J.
 Provincial of the Province of the Philippines
 February 2, 1977
Nihil Obstat:
 Rt. Rev. Msgr. Benjamin L. Marino, P.A.
 Vicar General - Chancellor
Imprimatur:
 ✠Jaime Cardinal L. Sin, D.D.
 Archbishop of Manila
 January 24, 1977

© 1977 by Ave Maria Press, Notre Dame, Indiana 46556

Library of Congress Catalog Card Number: 77-83197

International Standard Book Number: 0-87793-135-6 (Cloth)
                                    0-87793-136-4 (Paperback)

Cover photo: Candida Photos, Inc.
Design and typography: Cae Esworthy

Printed and bound in the United States of America.

Contents

Preface

This book has been "germinating" for several years. The encouragement to write it came from many friends in the Philippines and elsewhere—sisters, priests, seminarians and laity—who urged me to put in writing what I have been sharing with them on prayer in retreats, in lectures, in my course on "Apostolic Prayer," and in private direction. The opportunity to meet their request came when I was granted a sabbatical leave by the Provincial of the Jesuits in the Philippines, Rev. Benigno A. Mayo, S.J., and the authorities of the Loyola School of Theology of the Ateneo de Manila University.

During the months spent in the actual composition of the book, I have been greatly helped by discussions about its content with my mother and other friends. Two people have given it an especially close reading, and have made a number of suggestions to improve it, both in content and in clarity of expression: Sister Mary Ellen Doyle, of the Sisters of Charity of Nazareth, Kentucky, and my own sister, Marie Green James. To complete the family involvement in the project, my niece, Miss Peggy Green, carried through the thankless task of deciphering my handwriting and typing the manuscript. Sister Sheila, Sister Francis Mary, and the St. Joseph Sisters of Sacred Heart Cathedral Convent have generously handled the initial reproduction of the text, and Sister John Miriam Jones, S.C., Assistant Provost of the University of Notre Dame, has helped in exploring the possibilities of publication. Mr. Eugene Geissler, Book Editor of Ave Maria Press, has been a wise and understanding guide for my first venture into the mysterious world of book publishing.

One man on whom I counted to test the Spirit in these pages was Father Jim McCann, S.J., the latest of the three great directors whom the Lord has given me. Unfortunately for me, he died in Manila just a week before my return to the Philippines, so I never had the chance to share this adventure in grace with him. Until eternity, I shall have to be satisfied with the knowledge that the mark of his influence is in every chapter which follows.

It has been my hope that the Lord would use this book to say whatever *he* wanted to say. Thus, if there is any good in the book it is due, first of all, to the God and Father of our Lord Jesus, for he is, after all, the "Lord of the dance"; and then to all those, on various continents and islands, who have been praying for the project and who have shared the experience of their inner life with me. I owe a special debt to the men of San Jose Seminary. They have made life as a child of the third culture a real adventure in grace for me. It is really their book—their experience is the proof of whatever is true in these pages—and to them, and to Jim McCann who brought me to them and taught me to love them, I gratefully dedicate it.

Manila, Philippines
July 31, 1977
Feast of St. Ignatius Loyola

Introduction:
One Bread at Many Tables

In recent times, sociologists have sought to explain some of the phenomena of our shrinking world in terms of a "third culture." The concept is different from, although not entirely unrelated to, the much more common idea of the Third World. When two cultures meet, from whatever world they come, we are told that a third culture is formed at the point of intersection. For example, the British colonial administrator, who spent many years in India, was changed by his experience. While not really becoming Indian, he was also no longer wholly British. And the Indian civil servant with whom he worked was similarly changed, for better or worse, by his experience at the meeting of two worlds. The Englishman who returned home after many years in India would not find himself really at home in his native land. Nor would he be totally at home in a completely Indian milieu. He is a child of a new world, formed from the interaction of two living cultures, as is the black student of talent who is transplanted from the streets of Harlem to the gracious campus of an Ivy League university.

He may never feel really at home in the white world of the Ivy League, but he also discovers that, psychologically, he cannot go home to Harlem again. He, too, is a child of the intersection of two worlds.

I am not competent to pass judgment on the sociological merits of the third-culture concept. I mention it, however, because it has been of great help to me, personally, in understanding my own situation, and in seeing the meaning and place of prayer in the Christian life. I am a child of a third-culture myself, born and raised in the United States and called to live out my life as a missionary in the Philippines. Who am I really? To cling to my "Americanism" in an alien culture would be a certain formula for frustration and ineffectiveness. To seek to become wholly Filipino would mean reverting to the womb and living over again my whole history—an impossible task. The attempt would guarantee a nervous breakdown. Who am I then? Am I rootless, or am I rooted in two soils at once?

In this day and age, when the missionary can no longer even try to transplant a "little piece of America" to alien soil, these questions can provoke a real identity crisis. But it is also possible, thank God, that they be productive, although not without pain, of a real personal deepening and enrichment. The child of the third culture has a unique perspective. He can, if he has the eyes, begin to discern the constant and fundamental human values which underlie all concrete cultural embodiments of these values. He can discover his real roots as a human being. And he can wonder at, and be enriched by, the very diversity of expression of these roots.

This brings us to the topic of this book, for I have discovered that one of these constant and fundamental human values—and indeed the most important—is prayer. I have had occasion to move back and forth between my two worlds. It never ceases to amaze me that I hear the same questions about prayer in a convent in the isolated province of Antique by the Sulu Sea and in a convent at the Cathedral in Rochester, New York. The seminarians of San Jose in Manila and the seminarians of St. Bernard's in Rochester are confronted by the same problem of integrating prayer and service in the following of Christ. God reveals himself in essentially the same way to a lady dentist in Quezon City and a philosophy teacher in Columbus, Ohio, to a parish priest in Hornell and in Cavite.

This book, in fact, is born of that cross-cultural experience. Working as a director of souls in Antique and Rochester, in Columbus, Ohio, and Quezon City (and in Sydney and Singapore and Kuala Lumpur), I have found that the principal concern people share with me is their life of prayer. This has been a great challenge to me, for it has forced me to reflect constantly on the way God works in my life and in the lives of those I direct. It has driven me back, again and again, to the Church's masters of prayer, and to my own experience as a pray-er these past 25 years. And it has made me realize that there are certain common patterns of the interior life which transcend time and space —which are as valid in 1977 as in 1577, and in the Philippines as in the United States. This might have seemed self-evident 15 years ago, but it is by no means as obvious today in the light of the tremendous ferment in the Church after Vatican II. Tranquil assumptions, in prayer as in every other area of Christian life, have had to be subjected to searching reexamination.

Not Everyone Alike

The interior life, or the life of prayer, is a very mysterious reality. In one sense it just happens—to some people, apparently, and not to others—and there seems to be very little we can say to explain the mystery. Whether by temperament or family background or whatever, some people are "religious" and many more are not. When I was a boy, I had a great-aunt who had been educated by the ·

sisters in Canada. She was a sincere believer according to her own lights, but she would never consider herself religious. In fact, she used to recall that, in school, the sisters urged the girls to say three Hail Marys every day to pray for a religious vocation. And she never said the Hail Marys, because she was afraid she might get the vocation! If she were alive today, and were to read my book, she would be proud of me for having written it—but she would be convinced it was not for her. God, I am sure, played a very real part in her life; but there were limits to her involvement with him. Piety was for sisters, and for a few lay people. It was not for her.

What would have surprised my aunt is that not a few sisters probably felt as she did. They were committed to a life-style that was externally more pious. Yet, deep down, they had come to the conclusion that a real personal encounter with the Lord was not for them. More than once a good sister, long in the religious life, has told me that she was not called to be a pray-er. She never got anywhere in prayer, and she could only envy those around her who seemed to be on a first-name basis with the Lord. Reluctantly she (or rather they, since I have heard the story many times) had come to the conclusion that prayer was not for her. Whatever real prayer might be—whatever people around them who appeared caught up in the Lord might be experiencing—it was not part of their lives. They had no hope it ever would be, at least this side of the grave. If the Church be divided into queen bees who pray and worker bees who labor, their lot seemed clearly to be with the workers.

Desire to Pray Crucial

These sisters are in a somewhat different situation from my great-aunt: in a sense, she decided she didn't *want* to be religious; they would like to be, but it seems impossible to them. There are many lay people who would feel the same

15

way. They would like to know the Lord better, but the demands of their daily life and constant pressures of life in the world seem to make real growth in prayer impossible for them. Such people, whether religious or laity, are definitely among those for whom I write this book. The *desire* to pray is itself a clear sign of the Lord's presence. We cannot reach out to him unless he first draws us. Since he is Lord, since he cares more for us than we do for ourselves, he would never plant this desire in us merely to frustrate us. He would never lead us to seek something which was impossible.

How would this book be of help to such people— i.e., to people who would like to pray but who feel it is impossible for them, either because of their temperament or because of the circumstances of their lives? At first glance, the description of the way God works in prayer may seem too demanding for them. But certain points in the chapters that follow should be carefully noted.

In the first place, as Chapter 3 stresses, good prayer should not be divorced from daily life. To pray is *not* to withdraw from our daily concerns into some ethereal world. The religious person, in the true sense, is not someone who is out of touch with reality. Rather, good prayer means bringing our real concerns and responsibilities before the Lord and learning to hear what *he* has to say about them. What is not good—and this is the major point of Chapter 2 —is to look upon prayer as a way to manipulate God, to *use* him to accomplish our own desires.

God Speaks in Many Ways

This brings us to another important point. If only we have the ears to hear, God is speaking to us in all the events of our lives and not merely in times of formal prayer. Busy people will often say that their work is their prayer—a tricky slogan but one that contains an important grain of truth. It is true that everything that happens, everything that we do, is a revelation of God to us. But *not every revelation by God is a genuine encounter for us.*

How often have we had the experience of speaking to someone else and not being heard? We are speaking, revealing ourselves, but the other person is either not listening or is misunderstanding us. In Chapter 1, I stress that the art of listening is at the heart of genuine prayer. As we learn to listen with attention and sensitivity, all the events of our lives become encounters with the Lord, become prayer. That is why St. Ignatius Loyola, along with other great apostolic pray-ers, sees times of formal, systematic prayer as much more important to beginners than to those who have already learned to be sensitive to the way God speaks. Ignatius speaks of the mature apostle as a contemplative in action, someone who can "seek God in all things." It is in this sense that everything—work and play and rest—becomes truly prayer for the *mature* pray-er.

To reach this level of sensitivity, however, takes time and effort. This is where "my work is my prayer" can be a misleading slogan and a smoke screen to conceal the lack of any real depth in our lives. Chapter 3 makes clear that discernment is an art, and like any art it is only learned by experience. An "introduction to prayer" is really a guide to the experience which can teach us this art. The techniques of coming to quiet (in Chapter 4), of positively disposing our spirits to hear the Spirit (in Chapter 5), and of taking those initial steps in "mental prayer" which I call meditation and contemplation in Chapter 6, are not intended as mechanical steps to guarantee successful prayer. They are not an abstract theory of prayer. Rather they are the distillation of the experiences of praying Christians over the centuries as reflected through the prism of my own experience as a pray-er and a spiritual director. They are good only insofar as they help interested readers to a greater sensitivity to the Lord speaking in the daily events, ordinary and not-so-ordinary, of their lives.

Book to Be Lived

It should be noted, however, that this places a special burden on the reader. Many books can be read for the vicarious experience or the information they provide us—and then can be set aside. They can divert us, distract us, provide a break from our responsibilities, without making any further demands on us. But an introduction to prayer is not like that. To read it properly takes years, because it must be lived, experienced. Each time it is reread it will say something new to us—because we read it from a new experiential base. This is what I myself have discovered with the basic guides of my own interior life, like Teresa of Avila's *Way of Perfection* and Leonard Boase's *The Prayer of Faith*.

I can't help wondering, as I write them, what my great-aunt would think of these lines. Hopefully she would be enlightened to see that pious or prayerful do not have to have the otherworldly connotations she gave to them. But would she really want to read this book? Would she want to get that involved in it—to take it as a guide to her own exploration of a world that might make too many demands on her? I don't know. If I could talk to her about it now, though, I would not soft-pedal the commitment such a book requires. I would, however, try to tell her that prayerful people are *real* people—down-to-earth and truly involved and very human. They pay a price, not in order to be divorced from reality but in order to live life fully. I would count on her sharp Irish wit to puncture my balloon if my piety was pompous or condescending or unreal!

Those Who Pray Spontaneously

Among my readers there will also be some who already find prayer an important part of their lives. They would not be "turned off" by prayer—either out of disinterest or out of frustration. But they might feel that prayer is a very simple thing for them, that it is something spontaneous and natural and not in need of any elaborate explanations or justification. Tevye, in *Fiddler on the Roof,* would appear, at first sight, to be such a man. He speaks spontaneously and unaffectedly to a God who is as real to him as his own wife, and with whom he is more at home than he is with his liberated daughters.

Tevye, while an unusual figure, is not unique. One of the stories which made a great impression on me in my youth was about Jimmy, the laborer. Jimmy was a simple man, of little formal education. Each day, when returning from work, he stopped in the church and sat in the back for several minutes. The parish priest noticed the regularity of Jimmy's visits, and his fervor. He wondered just what a simple man like Jimmy did during these visits. One day he asked him what happened. Jimmy replied: "Nothing much, Father. I just say 'Jesus, it's Jimmy.' And he says 'Jimmy, it's Jesus.' And we're happy to be together."

What could be simpler or more spontaneous than Jimmy's encounter with the Lord? What could a book on prayer do for Jimmy except complicate a very real and deep, spontaneous relationship? The answer, of course, is that Jimmy's relationship to God *is* very deep and nothing should be done to complicate it or confuse it. No director, and no manual, can tell us how we *must* grow. Prayer is experienced and is utterly personal. There is no single method of prayer and no *one* way to encounter God. If Jimmy has found the Lord in his simplicity, then his way of arriving there is the right way for him.

This is a point which needs to be stressed. Four centuries ago, St. John of the Cross, one of the great spiritual directors of all time, wrote that the three great enemies of interior growth are the devil, oneself—*and the spiritual director!*[1] While he discusses the danger from the devil and

---

[1] *The Living Flame of Love,* Stanza III, par. 29-63.

from oneself in about two paragraphs each, he spends some 30 paragraphs on the danger from the spiritual director. Why? His point is, very simply, that most directors over-direct. They try to mold their directees according to their own experience or their own theories of prayer. For John, and for every good spiritual director, the director's role is not to mold souls according to some preconceived pattern, but to help them to interpret *their own* experience. The good director helps people to be free to follow the Lord in whatever way *he* chooses to lead them. We will discuss this point further in Chapter 3, when we speak of discernment—but note, for the moment, that "director" is not really a very happy title for the spiritual director. He would more aptly be called a "codiscerner."

To return to Jimmy and our question about the value of this book for him: it is clear from what we have said that nothing should be done to complicate Jimmy's relationship with the Lord. Yet, I think our Jimmy story may be misleading in its simplicity. Spiritual life, like all life, is growth and change. Jimmy has a history. He arrived at where he is now via a long process of joy and suffering, of doubt, perhaps, and testing. We don't know his history, but the story derives its depth of meaning from our own experience, our own history. Jimmy is a striking figure precisely because we know how rare and difficult such simple faith is for anyone who has really lived life with his eyes open. Jimmy may not need this book at the present point in his life with God. But Jimmy's story is told—and was told when I first heard it—not to canonize him but to move the hearer to desire to arrive where Jimmy is.

How does one, beginning where most of us begin a life of prayer—preoccupied, self-centered, and yet desirous of something better—come to such a real and simple experiential faith? To this question the book does try to provide an answer. Our hypothetical Jimmy might not need such an answer. But the apostles did, as is clear from their request,

when Jesus was at prayer, that he teach them to pray
(Lk 11:1). He had already given them numerous instruc-
tions on prayer and had taught them by his own example,
but they still felt they did not really know how to pray. They
needed help, and so do we.

Always "On the Way"

There is another sense in which our story about Jimmy
needs amplification. We said that spiritual life, like all life,
involves growth and change. Jimmy has a history. He has
come from somewhere—and *he is going somewhere*. Whatever his present experience of God may be, he still must
grow. In this life we are always "on the way." St. Paul says:
"Now we are seeing a dim reflection in a mirror; but then
(in eternity) we shall be seeing face to face. The knowledge
that I have now is imperfect; but then I shall know as fully
as I am known" (I Cor 13:12). No matter how deep our
experience of God is, we are always just beginning to know
the Lord. As Job, called the most godly man on the face of
the earth (Job 1:8), says at the end of his testing, "I had
heard of you by the hearing of the ear, but only now does
my eye see you" (Job 42:5). Even though he was the
godliest of the sons of men, he was really only beginning
to know the Lord.

Tevye, who in a sense is a modern Job, illustrates my
point well. *Fiddler on the Roof* begins with Tevye on easy
and intimate terms with the Lord. But the play itself is an
allegory of the purification of Tevye which John of the Cross
calls the dark night of the senses. His world collapses. His
final flight from the ancestral home in Anatenka is a symbol
of the erosion of the traditional values which had made his
life meaningful and his faith secure. To continue to encounter God as his world collapses will require much more
of Tevye than a simplistic "whistling in the dark" kind of
faith. Even the proficient pray-er of simple depth must grow,
and at times that growth will entail a "shaking of the

21

foundations." At times like that, I would hope this book would offer sounder guidance than Job received from his "friends."

Time of Transition

I was ordained a priest on the same day that Paul VI was elected pope. This has been a significant coincidence for me because it symbolized to me that I am truly a child of transition. My own religious formation, thoroughly traditional in the early years of the seminary, was profoundly influenced by the new winds which the great Pope John XXIII, as the instrument of the Spirit, sent blowing through the Church. The early years of my priesthood reflected, in a small way, the heroic struggle of Pope Paul VI to be open to all that is genuine in *aggiornamento* while, at the same time, remaining firmly rooted in faith. The changes consequent upon Vatican II—the renewed stress on community, both in liturgy and in the living of the Christian life, the stress on finding Christ in others and on the social dimension of the Gospel—did not produce a personal crisis in me. In fact, they appealed to me as liberating and enriching, as a much-needed expression of the personal commitment to the Lord which had come to define my vocation for me.

These changes have, however, had a significant impact on my work as a director of souls. Many pray-ers of my generation, as well as older generations, either questioned the relevance of their own formation and their own view of prayer and spiritual direction, or they clung to the old and rejected the new—or they were confused and troubled by the conflict between old and new. For a younger generation the problem was somewhat different. Very often they had not learned to pray as we had. Their approach was much more free-form, unstructured. They saw prayer as too personal to be governed by the methods on which an older generation relied. They came to maturity with a strong sense of social concern, and were impatient with and intolerant of any "me and Jesus" spirituality. They saw the latter as too egocentric, too self-indulgent to be tolerated as the world burned around them.

In my work as a director, I have had to deal with both young and old (and those in between) on both sides of the world. My directees have been a representative mix of ages and temperaments. They have been laity and religious and parish priests. But they are *not* a cross section of the general population. They had one concern in common: they cared enough about learning to pray, or continuing to grow in prayer, to seek direction and to share with me their inner lives. It is important to note this, because it is for them that this book is written. Whether priests or laity or religious, they want to learn to pray.

One final word is in order, concerning the use of books on prayer. Such a book is much more like a cookbook than like a novel or a treatise on economics. We read it not in order to be informed or vicariously moved, but in order to be guided in our action. No normal person, I presume, simply reads a cookbook from cover to cover for the enjoyment of reading it. While this book has, I hope, more unity and continuity than the average cookbook, it too is meant to be lived, acted upon, and not just read. Some parts of this book, or any book on prayer, may not speak to the reader's needs here and now. They can be skipped over lightly. Other parts will touch upon and illuminate points which do speak to one's present experience. They should be read and reread, and tested in the living of what they say.

Thus, the purpose of this book is to *describe* the life of prayer, at least in its initial stages, for those who truly want to learn to pray. It thus attempts to be not an attempt to convince the doubter of the value of prayer (necessary and valuable as such a book might be today), nor a suggested technique or techniques for praying (as I shall say later, I don't believe there are any such), but what might be called today a *phenomenology* of prayer—i.e., a *description* of the way the Lord actually seems to work, and the type of response he seems to desire, in the lives of men and women to whom he chooses to reveal himself. It would thus be a "justification" or "defense" of prayer only in the sense that what is described might move someone, under grace, to seek to experience for himself the same encounter in his own life. It is true that in the first part of the book I do discuss the question of the relevance and irrelevance of prayer. But this is done not in a way designed to convince the skeptic, but rather to help the convinced beginner to understand better the need he or she already feels to learn to pray. It is "faith in search of understanding," *fides quaerens intellectum.*

I believe, in fact, that experience is the only proof for such realities as prayer and love. The wife cannot really prove to someone else that her husband loves her. Every bit of evidence she presents can be explained in some other way ("He treats you tenderly because it is cheaper than having to hire a housekeeper!"). But she *knows, by experience,* that he loves her. Similarly, St. John says that he and Andrew first followed the Lord by the lakeshore at the bidding of John the Baptist.

> And Jesus turned, and saw them following, and said to them, "What do you seek?" And they said to him, "Rabbi" (which means Teacher), "where are you staying?" He said to them, "Come and see." They came and saw where he was staying; and they stayed with him that day, for it was about four o'clock in the afternoon. (Jn 1:38-39)

John rarely mentions the time of day in his Gospel, but this was the moment when he fell in love. If you asked John to prove that Jesus is Lord, I believe John would say: "The only proof is this. If you go to the shore of a certain lake at four in the afternoon, you may see what I saw. If you do, you will know that Jesus is Lord." The only proof is experience.

I

The What and Why of Prayer

1

What Prayer Is

For the past several years, I have been a spiritual director in a major seminary. The spiritual director's job is a unique one for which there seems to be no real training except experience. He is a curious mix: an *alter ego,* or other self, sharing with young people what is most precious and most private to them—their own inner selves; he is something of a guru, from whom they hope to learn their secret mantra; he is a strong shoulder in their troubled times and a sounding board for their hopes and plans. In all this, it seems to me, the spiritual director is above all a listener. The hardest thing he has to learn is truly to listen, not passively but creatively and responsively.

The importance, and difficulty, of listening were brought home forcefully to me on one occasion. A fine seminarian was beginning a directed retreat. He was somewhat quiet, and I, in my usual style, wanted to put him at ease and draw him out. When we met in the evening to discuss how the first day had gone, I began to ask him about his experience. He cut me short by saying: "Before we

start, I'd like to ask one favor." "What is that?" I asked.
He said: "Whenever you start talking, I get nervous and
forget what I wanted to say. So please don't say anything
until I have finished sharing what I want to share." For
the next several days I successfully (heroically!) held my
tongue—and since then I have found that, for me, talker
that I am, learning to listen well has demanded much personal discipline.

As I reflect on those years of learning to listen, I
realize that the very effort to do so has taught me more
about prayer than any other aspect of my priestly ministry
—both because the art of listening seems to me to be at the
very heart of prayer, and because prayer itself has been the
central topic which the seminarians have wanted to talk
about. There are many problems which arise: family,
studies, vocation, celibacy, community. But the continually
recurring theme in our conversations is prayer. The basic
question is: Just what is prayer? We can't really talk about
how to do it unless we have some definite idea of what it is.

Those of us who are old enough to have been raised
on the Baltimore Catechism (and its counterparts) learned
early in life to define prayer as a lifting of the mind and
heart to God. This was an easy definition to memorize—
clear and brief. It was a good definition in that it taught us
that (1) God is far beyond our ordinary experience; (2)
prayer entails effort on our part; and (3) prayer involves
both the mind and the heart—the understanding and the
feelings and will—of man. If we explore these three elements of the catechism definition a little further, perhaps
we can come to a clearer picture of just what prayer should
be.

The last point—the place of the heart in prayer—
is an important one, and one that has not always been so
clear. For many of the desert fathers and theologians of the
early Church, perhaps largely under the influence of Greek
philosophy, prayer was primarily a matter of the understanding, of knowledge. As such it was very much like

27

theology, which sought to place reason at the service of faith—to use reason to understand and clarify the divine revelation. The theologian and the pray-er differed not so much in what they did—both were knowers—as in the means they used to achieve knowledge. The theologian employed his *natural* faculties of reason and reflection, while the pray-er, in this early tradition, employed esoteric or secret techniques which were supposed to lead to a privileged, supernatural, "mystical" way of knowing God and understanding ultimate reality.

This view of prayer and spirituality was condemned by the Church as heretical very early in her history. Its major defect, however, was not its stress on the understanding to the relative neglect of the heart.[1] The really fatal flaw in these early theories of prayer pertained more to the second of the three points we noted above, namely that prayer entails effort on our part. It was condemned because of its *excessive* reliance on man's own efforts. In the partisan terminology of the times, it was found to be "Pelagian" or "semi-Pelagian," i.e., to follow the theologian Pelagius in overestimating man's ability to encounter God by his own efforts and to neglect the absolute primacy of God's grace. There is an infinite chasm between God and man; man, no matter how hard he tries, cannot come to God—cannot

---

[1]Almost a thousand years later St. Thomas Aquinas, one of the greatest pray-ers and greatest theologians in the history of the Church, would still be very much in the intellectualist tradition (i.e., emphasizing man's understanding in prayer). And 300 years later still Martin Luther would react against a predominantly intellectualist Catholic view of faith. It is true that a one-sided, exclusive stress on the understanding would be rare after the fifth century. But, despite the Franciscan emphasis on the will and on love, the primacy of man's intellect or understanding had a long history; and it is probably no exaggeration to say that the Catholic tradition of prayer is much indebted to Luther and the great Protestant thinkers who followed him—as much as to any human agency—for the emphasis on the heart in recent centuries. Luther, in turn, felt greatly indebted to the spiritual theology of St. Bernard of Clairvaux.

leap across infinity.[2] He cannot even, as the semi-Pelagians maintained, take the first step in coming to God. God must come to man. He alone can leap the infinite gulf between creator and creature; this is what he did in the Incarnation of Jesus and what he does in the life of every pray-er who truly encounters him.

Although it is easy enough to label this idea semi-Pelagian, and thus to relegate it to the dustbin of history, I am afraid the real situation is not as simple as that. As I look at my own years of learning to pray, it seems clear that there was a good bit of the semi-Pelagian in me, too. The structures within which I was formed as a religious tended to reinforce this stress on a "pulling-myself-up-by-my-bootstraps" kind of spirituality. The format of our novitiate times of prayer (about which I will have some positive things to say later) was rigidly prescribed. Point books provided structured meditations; some 60 of us novices meditated in one room; the one acceptable posture was kneeling. If someone was not kneeling during prayer, he could expect a summons from the director of novices and an inquiry whether he was ill. I quaked through a few of these encounters myself; at the time, while I dreaded them, I came to see them as developing manliness and self-discipline. Later I came to resent the regimentation they implied. Later still, when I myself began to direct souls, I realized that these practices were all part of a widespread spirit of an age:[3] asceticism, self-denial, killing one's own

---

[2]This was the first of the three elements we noted in the catechism definition of prayer.

[3]The pendulum has swung very far to the other side in just 20 years, and the catchwords have now become "self-expression," "personal fulfillment," "doing my own thing." Since this extreme is even more harmful to a solid spirituality, we shall have to discuss, in Chapter 5, the positive value of asceticism in any genuine interior life. What we seek, throughout the book, is a balance between God's work and man's—a dialogue between grace and personal initiative.

will and desires were, in a sense, at the very core of spirituality. It was as if Jesus' mysterious saying "Since John the Baptist came, up to this present time, the kingdom of heaven has been subjected to violence and the violent are taking it by storm" (Mt 11:12) had been appropriated, alone and out of context, as the basis for a whole spirituality.

The fruit of the semi-Pelagian controversy has been to make us realize that our own effort is utterly secondary to the work of God in our encounter with him. Yet I have felt for some time that this is still a defect in the catechism definition of prayer with which we began this chapter. The idea of *raising* our minds and hearts to God still seems to imply that prayer is largely a matter of our own efforts—that God is simply there, while we, in prayer, find ways and means to pull ourselves up to him. Such a view would obviously be semi-Pelagian, and hence unacceptable to the Christian.

Since Christians have recently shown much interest in Yoga and Zen and their derivatives, it is worth noting in this context that such a view (i.e., that prayer is totally, or largely, a matter of our own efforts) does find considerable support in the great Oriental religions such as Hinduism and Buddhism. In those Oriental traditions which do not know a personal God, prayer depends totally on the effort of the pray-er—even if that effort is, paradoxically enough for the Westerner, wholly devoted to emptying the mind, to coming to quiet, to passivity. It is important to note, however, that even in the mainstream Oriental traditions—and particularly in the classical literature of Hinduism—there are affirmations of the personality of God and intimations of a doctrine of grace. In *The Bhagavad Gita,* "the Blessed One" says of his true disciples:

> To them, constantly disciplined,
> Revering Me with love,

I give that discipline of mind,
Whereby they go unto Me.[4]

There has been some dispute within Hinduism about
the literal meaning of texts like these.[5] But for us Christians,
there can be no doubt: God is a person (in fact, three Persons!), and prayer is a personal encounter with him. More
than that, it is an encounter which depends almost entirely
on his grace, since he is God.

This is not the place to attempt to explain to the
puzzled Christian what exactly lies at the end of the road
of prayer for the Hindu or Buddhist contemplative. My
point is simply that Christian prayer is grounded in a very
specific conception of God: a personal God who encounters his creatures in love. To return to the catechism
definition, the idea of prayer as a raising of our minds and
hearts to God seems to me to overstress our own effort and
activity in prayer. For some time, I have been suggesting
that a better approach would be to define prayer as an
opening of the mind and heart to God. This seems better
because the idea of opening stresses receptivity, responsive-
ness to another. To open to another is to act, but it is to
act in such a way that the other remains the dominant
partner.

Perhaps the clearest example of openness is the art of
listening, which we discussed at the beginning of this
chapter. Listening is indeed a real art, which some people
never learn. We all have experienced people who cannot or
do not listen. They hear but do not understand; their bodily
ears pick up sound, but their hearts are not attentive to its
meaning. You can talk *to* them, but you can scarcely talk
with them. Yahweh uses this image of hearing and yet not
hearing to express his frustration with Israel: "Hear this, O

---

[4]*The Bhagavad Gita,* translated by Franklin Edgerton, Chapter
X, stanza 10 (p. 51). Harvard University paperback, 1972.
[5]See, for example, K. M. Sen, *Hinduism* (Pelican paperbacks,
1970), pp. 20, 74, 91.

foolish and senseless people, who have eyes, but see not, who have ears, but hear not" (Jer 5:21); and Jesus uses it to the same effect when speaking of his own "hearers" after the multiplication of the loaves: "Why do you discuss the fact that you have no bread? Do you not yet perceive or understand? Are your hearts hardened? Having eyes do you not see, and having ears do you not hear? And do you not remember?" (Mk 8:17-18).

Hearing or listening is a good metaphor for prayer. The good pray-er is above all a good listener. Prayer is dialogue; it is a personal encounter in love. When we communicate with someone we care about, we speak and we listen. But even our speaking is responsive: What we say depends upon what the other person has said to us. Otherwise we don't have real dialogue, but rather two monologues running along side by side.

I believe that our remarks have carried us a good way toward understanding what prayer is. In the past we have catalogued prayer under four headings: *a*doration, *c*ontrition, *t*hanksgiving and *s*upplication (or petition)—easy to remember because the initial letters spell "acts." This is helpful in that it makes clear that there is much more to prayer than merely asking for things (supplication). But we have seen that we need to go deeper than "acts" of our own to get to the real meaning of prayer. Prayer is essentially a dialogic encounter between God and man; and since God is Lord, he alone can initiate the encounter. This is the important implication of the first element of our catechism definition. Hence what man does or says in prayer will depend on what God does or says first. Here, above all, it is true that "You have not chosen me; I have chosen you" (Jn 15:16). God's choice, his call, is fundamental and all-important.

At the same time, prayer is a dialogue, an encounter between two persons. What man does or says is an integral part of prayer, since even God cannot speak *with* us unless we also speak. Even God cannot dialogue with a man who is interiorly deaf and mute. This was the second element of value in our catechism definition: Prayer does entail effort on the part of man, even though it is always God who reaches across infinity to us, and even though man's effort is itself impossible without the sustaining grace of God.

Moreover, as the third element of the catechism definition made clear, man's response involves both his head and his heart. The understanding plays an important role in prayer, since man cannot love what he does not know. His love is proportioned to his knowledge. At the same time, prayer is not mere reasoning or speculation about God. As Teresa of Avila says in the *Interior Castle,* "The important thing (in prayer) is not to think much but to love much."[6] The goal of prayer is the encounter with God in love. And love, as Teresa goes on to say "consists, not in the extent of our happiness, but in the firmness of our determination to try to please God in everything." Thus prayer involves the heart and will of man, even more fundamentally than his understanding.

It was St. Augustine, one of the greatest intellects the Church has produced, who said "Our hearts are restless until they rest in thee."[7] For the learned man fulfillment may lie in the mind's coming to rest, but for the pray-er, the lover, it is the heart that matters most.

In this connection, it is important to note that *spontaneity* is of the very essence of prayer, as it is of all dialogue. Augustine's "heart" is a spontaneous organ, responding to the sacrament of the present moment. Its responses cannot be programmed, because we cannot know in advance the word which God will speak to us at any given moment. When we were novices we were encouraged

---

[6]The Fourth Mansions, Chapter One (volume II, p. 233 in the translation by E. Allison Peers of *The Complete Works of St. Teresa of Jesus,* Sheed & Ward, 1946).

[7]*Confessions* of St. Augustine, Book I, Chapter 1, trans. Frank Sheed (Sheed & Ward, 1943) p. 3.

to plan our conversations for recreation—presumably so that the topics discussed would be fruitful and uplifting. The result, of course, was some very stilted conversations—and some very funny, though frustrating, encounters where each participant labored mightily to steer the talk to his own planned area. Since then I have heard the same thing at social events and cocktail parties, with the same ludicrous results. In the novitiate the intention was good, but the loss in spontaneity was disastrous. The same thing will be true in a programmed approach to prayer.

To the beginner, there is still a puzzle and a mystery in listening to God. (To the proficient pray-er it is no longer a puzzle, but it will always be a mystery.) Since we never encounter God in the same way we encounter another human being, how do we know when God talks? How do we interpret what he "says" when he does not speak as men speak? How can I respond meaningfully to someone whose coming is always veiled in the mystery of faith? In short, how do I know I am not just talking to myself when I pray? The central purpose of this book is to help to answer these questions—not in a way that will eliminate the mystery of faith, but in a way that will encourage the beginner to begin and to continue to discover God speaking in his or her own life.

We have based our explanation of what prayer is on the human experience of dialogue and listening. I think we will see, in the chapters that follow, that our ordinary human experience of love and dialogue—whether between husband and wife, between director and directee, or between friend and friend—can help us a great deal to discover and interpret our experience of prayer as a personal encounter in love between God and man.

2

The "Irrelevance" of Prayer

In the second part of the book, I will attempt to describe in fuller detail the way God normally works in the initial stages of the personal encounter with man which we call prayer. But first it might be helpful to consider certain questions which are often posed today, and which could be a block to the (prospective) beginner. One question, which we will discuss in this chapter, has to do with the "irrelevance" of prayer for the ordinary person: is not prayer, at least as we have described it, a luxury which the average layman, and even the average active priest or religious (active in the sense of being professionally committed to serving their fellowmen and preaching the gospel in the marketplace) can ill afford? Are we not talking about something exotic and unreal in a world where social justice, human rights, and even the basic demands of family and job, require of most people more energy than they have? These are real questions today. I have been asked them by seminarians in Manila, who felt that responding to the needs of the poor in the slums near the seminary was far more pressing, and far more Christian, than spending time wrapped up in their own private prayer life. The same questions have been put to me by parents of young families, who could not even find the time and quiet space to talk to one another, to say nothing of finding time and space for prayer.

This last difficulty suggests that we would do well to explore the analogy of human love in seeking an answer to our question about the relevance of prayer. A husband and wife who don't have time for each other may be heading for serious trouble, whatever their reasons for this lack of time. Similarly, a couple who sought to justify their intimacy solely in terms of its usefulness in raising the children could be heading for difficult times. Imagine the relationship between a husband and wife who truly love each other.[1] They live for each other day by day. There are good days and bad days, but both are part of a relationship which deepens with the years and gives meaning to both their lives. There are moments of intimacy when they are able to experience and to express all that they mean to each other.

Suppose that it is such a moment of deeper intimacy. They are filled with the joy of their love for each other. Suddenly a troubling thought comes to the wife, and she is moved to voice it out. "What," she asks her husband, "is the *relevance* of our love for each other?" What a queer question that would· be at such a time! He would be puzzled, surprised, irritated perhaps. The mood of their loving encounter would be broken.

Why? Because love is *not* relevant—timely, opportune, pertinent, useful. Once lovers begin to ask these questions their love has become an object to be examined and not an experience to be lived. And love objectified is love distorted —the very thought of it makes uncomfortable those who have known love.

---

[1]Caryl Houselander and Rosemary Haughton, two of the best "spiritual writers" of our time, have both explored some of the implications of this analogy. See Houselander's *This War Is the Passion* and Haughton's *The Transformation of Man.*

It is the same way with the love of God. If we try to analyze it like a watch or a scientific problem, we destroy it or distort it. If we try to determine its relevance, to justify it by showing that it is useful, it slips through our fingers. Love is a splendidly useless passion—whether it be the love of man or the love of God. Love is the thing, *par excellence,* which, in the happy phrase of Wittgenstein, cannot be said but can only be shown. The experience itself is the only proof, the only justification. That, perhaps, is why proofs for God's existence always seem unsatisfactory: for the unbeliever, they don't prove (only experience can); and for the believer they fall far short of the reality of his experience.

Since we have described prayer as a love relationship with God, the pray-er faces the same problem as the wife. Prayer is not to be used but to be lived. Either the experience of God in prayer is its own justification or no justification is possible. For the beginner this can pose a special problem, at least if he comes to prayer not because he experiences God drawing him, but because he or she (for example, as a seminarian or as a novice in a congregation of sisters) is told that he or she should pray. It would seem difficult, from what we have said, to provide an argument why a beginner—who has not experienced prayer—should try to pray. Judging from my experience, this is true. Often beginners are drawn to pray because they have had some previous experience of the joy of knowing God. But it is increasingly common today that young men and women enter the seminary or the novitiate not because they desire to know God but because they desire to serve their fellowman. The Church, thank God, seems to many a good channel for their desire to serve—but the personal knowledge of Christ on which the Church's mission is grounded (see I Jn 1:1-4) is vague and unreal to them. They are quite at home with talk about "finding Christ in others" as long as no one raises the question just *who* Christ is for them. Concern about knowing God, encountering Christ, praying, seems an unnecessary, and even sinful, self-indulgence in a disjointed and fragmented world. Granted the point of our analogy to human love's irrelevance, what right do we have to waste time on the irrelevant in this day and age?

Is this true? Is prayer a luxury, exotic and unreal in today's pressurized and shrinking world? The question has a special urgency in the third world today, with its wide gulf between rich and poor and its relative lack of a middle class. The average Christian worker earns very little (in the range of $1.00 to $2.00 a day), has a large family (often six to eight children), and works six days a week. And the average apostle—priest, sister, brother or lay apostle—is overwhelmed by the demands of bringing a measure of social justice and development to such a desperate situation. What time or energy would such a worker, or such an apostle, have for a personal encounter with God?

The situation is by no means as desperate in the developed world. But the problem is there. Parkinson's law holds true, that the work (and problems) expand to fill the time available. Even the Rockefellers probably feel that they have trouble making ends meet, and most people in a developed society feel far less secure than the Rockefellers. Consumerism, which has been the wellspring of development, must continually create new needs in order to survive. The media create the needs (and they become all too real to those who feel them) and credit cards postpone the day of reckoning. Again, in such a climate, what time or energy would the average worker, or the average apostle (who breathes the air of consumerism every bit as much as his brethren), have for a personal encounter with God?

These questions can be answered in several ways. Perhaps the first thing that we must recall is that *God* is the initiator of the encounter which we call prayer. Jesus says, "You have not chosen me; I have chosen you" (Jn 15:16). St. Paul, in his Epistle to the Romans (8:14-34), gives magnificent expression to the fact that it is the Spirit of God who works in us—not only to justify us but also to teach us how to speak to God; that, in fact, "we do not know how to pray as we ought; but the Spirit himself makes intercession for us with groanings which cannot be expressed in speech. And he who searches hearts knows what the Spirit means, for the Spirit intercedes for the saints as God himself wills" (Rom 8:26-27).

Thus the encounter with the Lord is primarily his work, and since "the Spirit breathes where he wills" (Jn 3:8), the experience of prayer can occur in what, for us, are most unpromising situations and to most unlikely persons. God is the Lord; "The Spirit is not bound" by events, by social situations—a freedom which Jesus exercised magnificently in appearing first to Mary Magdalene, "from whom he had cast out seven demons" (Mk 16:9), on the morning of the Resurrection. What the late Bishop Ian Ramsey has called "disclosure situations," events of our concrete experience which suddenly become revelations of the presence and love of God, can occur most unexpectedly: on a bus, while watching TV, in ordinary conversation. I have had the experience of vainly seeking God throughout a fruitless hour of prayer, only to suddenly hear his voice or feel his presence in the sunset or in the passing word of a friend, or even while preparing a class lecture on a topic quite unrelated to prayer.

But, one may ask, does this really answer our question of relevance? Are we not simply saying that God is a law unto himself and our worldly concerns are really of no value? This would be to say, in effect, that our question of relevance is itself irrelevant. Such an interpretation has, indeed, had a long and vigorous history in the Church, in both Protestant and Catholic traditions. I hope to show shortly that it is mistaken, at least in being too one-sided; but we must acknowledge that it has a solid grounding in scripture. From the beginning of Israel's history as the people of God, Yahweh insisted that he was different from the gods of the Gentiles: He could not be manipulated by men; he was not simply a human being with all the foibles of men, like the Homeric and Canaanite gods. He was the totally other, so far beyond the comprehension of men that they could not even name him (Ex 3:13ff). In the book of Job, the answer to the problem of suffering is that God's providence is to be trusted, not explained. And Jesus makes abundantly clear that, in the New Covenant, too, the ways of God are not the ways of men. This is clear, for example, in his response to the complaint of Judas about the waste of the precious ointment (Jn 12:3-8). Similarly, one of the best descriptions I have found for the primary task of the pray-er is "learning to waste time gracefully."

What, then, can we say about the relevance of prayer —or, for that matter, of religion? Given the biblical picture of God's otherness (his transcendence)—given that "his ways are not our ways"—it would seem that it is misleading, at best, to speak of prayer as relevant. In an important sense, I believe this is true. If by revelant we mean a useful means to accomplish ends which we determine for ourselves, then, I believe, it is a serious distortion of prayer (and religion) to treat it as relevant. That is the flaw in much of what we actually call prayer. Jesus teaches us to say, "Thy will be done." If we are honest with ourselves, we know that most of the time what we really say is, "My will be thine, O Lord." That is, we make up our minds what is really best —a job, health, security, love—and then we beg the Lord to bring about what we want. Prayer as a means to accomplish our ends is indeed a very limited relevance; God, being God, simply cannot be manipulated to our ends.

To summarize what we have been saying in this chapter, there is an important sense in which prayer is, and must be irrelevant. If by relevant we mean useful as a means to accomplish our ends, then prayer is no more relevant than is human love. "Fall in love, get married, have a friend, because it will make you a more useful member of society."

Such advice sounds queer—and even indecent, to one who has known by experience the meaning of love and friendship. Adolescents do indeed seek friends to bolster their own self-image, to reassure themselves that they are OK. But as they become adults they quickly realize the difference between real friendship and being used. They resent it when others are friendly only when and because they want something. They feel guilty if they catch themselves behaving the same way.

The same thing is true in our relationship to God. The death of God theologians of the 1960's criticized conventional religion for worshiping a "god of the gaps," a god who was merely a need-fulfiller and problem-solver. Their point was that most people simply use God as a last resort when their own resources fail them. He is a *deus ex machina,* as he was for the classical dramatists, who is trotted out only to resolve situations (saving a country, healing sickness, passing an exam) which have become humanly impossible to resolve. In our terms, most people try to make God and prayer relevant in the wrong sense; they want to know how prayer can be useful to them in living their lives.

In opposition to this view we have said that: 1) love and friendship are not means but ends, and hence prayer, which is our love-relationship to God, cannot be relevant in the sense that we simply use it, whether to change the world or to achieve peace of heart; and 2) prayer is unique among human relationships in that it is a relationship to God, who is the unutterably Holy One and hence always remains the master of the encounter, who cannot be used or manipulated by man. In this sense it is correct to say that prayer is supremely irrelevant.

There is, however, another sense in which prayer is supremely relevant. If we think of relevance as measured, not in terms of our own social or personal goals, but rather in terms of God's creative work in the world, then the focus of our question is altered. Now it is no longer a question whether prayer can be shown to be revelant to those goals which we set for ourselves and for society. Rather the question is whether prayer can be shown to be relevant to our search for God's designs for us and the world. Can we know without prayer what is the will of God for us? If not, can prayer enable us to discern his will and to follow it? These are the questions to which we now turn.

3

The Relevance of Prayer: Discernment

In what sense can prayer be said to be supremely relevant to the life of man in the world? To answer concretely, let us suppose that a father of a family or a young religious is truly committed to "doing God's will" in his or her life—that he or she is convinced that God is the Lord of history, that he cares about his people and involves himself in their destiny.[1] In that case, the question arises: How do I discover God's will for his people, for me? Very often in the past, committed Catholics have answered this question for themselves by an appeal to authority. I know God's will for me by listening to those through whom God speaks: the pope, the bishop, the parish priest, civil authorities, parents. To discover God's will for me I simply have to listen to them.

---

[1]Recall that this is the reader for whom this book is written. To make faith reasonable to the unbeliever is a very important part of the Church's mission, but this task would require a separate, and a very different, book from the present one.

There is truth here. God has chosen to speak through men, a wondrous truth which finds its grounding and its climactic expression in the Incarnation of the Son of God. Jesus himself affirmed the fact that God speaks to men through other men, even in the critical situation where the authoritative mouthpieces of God are unworthy of their calling. In St. Matthew's Gospel (Mt 23:1-3), Jesus begins a scathing denunciation of the scribes and Pharisees by saying to the crowds and to his disciples: "The scribes and the Pharisees sit on Moses' seat (i.e., have inherited the authority of Moses to lead God's chosen people); so practice and observe whatever they tell you, but not what they do; for they preach but do not practice."

That God should have spoken through the mouth of a jackass (Num 23) is wondrous enough; that he should choose to speak through the mouths of evil men[2] is more remarkable still. There is, in fact, probably no greater test of the faith of the believer. Such faith would, I suspect, be impossible for the reflective believer unless he were a man of prayer.

Granted this faith, however, and granted the necessity of prayer to sustain it, what are we to say of discovering God's will in our lives? Is it simply a question of listening to those, be they good or bad, through whom the Lord chooses to speak authoritatively? No, it is not as simple as that—and for two reasons. In the first place, the spokesman of God can only learn what he is to say by listening to God, by prayer. God *can* lead by blind guides, can speak through mouths that do not themselves comprehend what they are saying (see Jn 11:49-51 and 18:14). But such people also do great harm and will have much to answer for when their day of judgment comes.

Moreover, even *sincere* leaders—civil and religious, priests, sisters and laymen—fail in their "prophetic" (i.e.,

---

[2]If this seems too harsh a description, read the rest of Chapter 23 of Matthew to see what Jesus thought of certain scribes and Pharisees of his time.

45

speaking in the name of Yahweh) role if they are not men and women who listen to the Lord and are guided by him in their guidance of men. To seek to lead others by my own best lights is a commendable human act; but it is not prophetic, not priestly. The Epistle to the Hebrews puts it forcefully: "For every high priest chosen from among men is appointed to act on behalf of men in relation to God . . . And one does not take the honor upon himself, but he is called by God, just as Aaron was" (Heb 5:1,4). Much of the Old Testament is dominated by the conflict between the true and the false prophets (see, for example, I Kings, Isaiah, Jeremiah), and the point of the contrast between the two is clear: The true prophets listen to God and speak to men the word they hear from him; the false prophets do not.

This is the first reason why authority alone will not suffice to discover God's will: those in authority do not learn his will by some magical grace of office but by listening to him, by encountering him in prayer. There is also a second reason, which pertains not to authority as such but to what it means to be Christian. Most Christians are called to be mature, responsible adults. Their maturity and responsibility are not left at the Church door. Precisely as Christians they must discover God's will in their lives. Authority can help them (for example, by providing authentic guidelines on matters such as abortion, worship, social justice). But authority can never spell out *in detail* how an individual Christian should live his or her life.[3] Thank God such a use of authority is impossible; if it were possible, it would keep Christians in a state of perpetual preadolescence.

The average Christian is not called to this kind of perpetual childhood, but rather to be a mature man or

---

[3]St. Thomas Aquinas is very clear on this, in his discussion of the more general and the more specific principles of the natural law. See *Summa Theologiae* I-II, question 94, article 4.

woman in Christ. St. Paul was a strong personality and spoke with authority, and yet he continually exhorts his converts to realize the maturity to which they are called (see especially I Cor 14:20 and Eph 4:13-15). In the concrete, for Paul, this meant being able to recognize and follow the good spirit and to reject the evil spirit in the actual life-situations of the Christian in the world. Divinely constituted authority can provide authentic general guidelines for Christian action. A good spiritual director can help to interpret the way these guidelines apply to the concrete life-situation of an individual Christian. But the challenge remains for the Christian himself; he must make, and take personal responsibility for, the specific faith-decisions which determine the direction of his life. If these are truly to be *faith*-decisions, then the average Christian must also be able to recognize the Lord's will for him. He must open his mind and heart to God and be able to hear and understand the Lord's word. He must, in short, be a man of prayer.

Thus we have seen that prayer is truly relevant, both for the apostle *and* for the ordinary Christian, insofar as it is in prayer that we hear God and discover his will for us in the specific circumstances of our life. This link between prayer and action has been known in the Christian tradition as discernment.

Discernment is, in popular terms, an art and not a science—that is, it is learned only by doing. Like any artist, the person skilled in discernment finds it difficult to formulate rules to teach another person how to discern well. A skilled bicycle rider would find it hard to explain how he balances his weight on two small tires. When he began to ride, he was probably very unsteady and continually losing his balance. How did he master the bicycle? He could not say, except to tell us that "practice makes perfect." In fact, if he did try, while cycling, to analyze for himself how he manages the balancing act, he would probably get entangled in the wheels and fall off. Similarly, an experienced doctor would probably find it difficult to explain to an intern the reasoning process that led him to a successful diagnosis. A good insurance agent could not put into simple logical form the knowledge acquired through many years of experience in his profession.

Since discernment is the art of interpreting God's word to us and his will for us, the experience required is an experience of God—of his likes and dislikes, his desires for us and for the world. Perhaps the best analogy is, again, the experience of human love. When two people love each other, each becomes expert at interpreting the moods, the wishes, the hopes and fears of the other. A small example: I can remember, when my father was still living, going into a store to shop with my mother. We wanted to buy a necktie for Father's Day. The counter before us was filled with neckties, and yet my mother looked through them quickly and "instinctively" said: "No, he wouldn't like that one," . . . "Not that one either," . . . "Nor this," . . . "Ah, yes! This is the one he would like!" And she really meant: *"He* would like this"; not, "This is the one I like . . . The one *I* want him to like." How did she know? (She was right; he did like it!) Only by years and years of living together and sharing day by day.

Similarly, in our relationship with God the signs or touchstones of mature love are instinctive judgments about what would please him, instinctive sensitivity to the quiet word or small gesture which anyone except a lover would overlook. How does one come to such a union of hearts and wills? Only by years of fidelity and experience and reflection. Young lovers don't possess it. Beginners in prayer don't possess it, either. There is no shortcut to acquiring it.

We can, however, give some guidelines for the beginner. Let us begin from the question which all of us who pray ask ourselves at one time or another: When I pray, how do I know that it is God I am talking to and not just myself? I have been asked this question many times, by lay people and religious alike. One dedicated diocesan priest was particularly concerned about it; his work was demanding and challenging, and he did not want to be deluded into wasting precious time just talking to himself.

Normally, pray-ers do not have visions or hear mystical voices. We try to come to quiet—to get some distance from the noise and distractions of our busy lives—and to reflect on what the Lord wants of us. Certain ideas come to us: "I should try to be more attentive to my husband." "Perhaps I should be living a poorer life—after all, Jesus did not have a place to lay his head." "My coming to the novitiate was a mistake; God wants me to serve him in the lay state." The Lord normally does speak to us in this way—through our own ideas. But how do we know they are from God and not just from ourselves? How do we know they truly convey his will for us?

The question cannot be answered quickly and simply. This is why, in important matters, a good spiritual director is essential, especially for beginners. The role of the director is to be a codiscerner, to help us to interpret what God is saying to us in the concrete events of our lives. He or she should be someone experienced in the ways of God, *simpatico,* to whom we can be open and in whom we have confidence—someone, in short, whom we believe to be attuned to God and attuned to us.

Since a good director, however, is a *co*discerner, his or her task is not to tell us what to do but to help us to make our own sound judgments about God's word to us. A good director forms mature people, able to stand on their own spiritual feet. A book for beginners in prayer would not be the place for a full discussion of the what and how of discernment. But perhaps we can suggest a few basic rules which, in my experience, can be very useful even to the beginner.

(1) The basic touchstone of all good discernment is the *scripture.* For the Christian, God has revealed himself "by a Son, whom he appointed the heir of all things, through whom also he created the world" (Heb 1:2). Jesus

himself is the revelation of the Father to men. In his life we find the pattern of our lives as Christians, followers of Christ. Paul exhorted his followers to "be imitators of me, as I am of Christ" (I Cor 11:1). In his letter to the Galatians (2:20), he gives glorious expression to the mystical identification (and not merely imitation) with Jesus which is the essence of being Christian: "I have been crucified with Christ; it is no longer I who live, but Christ who lives in me; and the life I now live in the flesh I live by faith in the Son of God, who loved me and gave himself for me."

For the early Church, this sense of identification with Christ was very strong. As time passed, however, and more and more came to believe in Jesus who had never known him in the flesh, it became increasingly important to put in writing who Jesus was and what he stood for. For Peter and James and John, the memory of Jesus remained strong as long as they lived. For those who believed in him because of their preaching, but who had never walked the roads of Palestine with him, something more was needed. The original ending of St. John's Gospel makes clear that this was the *raison d'etre* of the scriptures, the reason why they were written. The final incident of John's Gospel[4] is the encounter between Jesus and "doubting Thomas," and Jesus' very last words are: "Blessed are those who have not seen and yet believe." *We* are the ones who have not seen and yet believe, and John concludes by explaining that it is for us that the Gospel has been written: "Now Jesus did many other signs in the presence of the disciples, which are not written in this book; but these are written that you may believe that Jesus is the Christ, the Son of God, and that believing you may have life in his name" (Jn 20:30-31).

---

[4]Chapter 21 was added later, although an original draft of much of it may well have been written by John. See verse 24 for evidence that it was added later and verse 23 for the reason why it was added. Contrary to the expectations of the early Church, John had died. His death seemed to belie a prediction which they thought Jesus had made to Peter.

Thus we come to know Jesus through the scriptures. To know God's will is basically to test our inspirations against the scriptures in which God is revealed to us through his Son. For this reason also, as we will explain more fully in Part II, the scriptures form the one essential "prayer book" for the meditation of the beginner.

(2) A second basic rule of discernment for the beginner is the following: for those who are sincerely seeking to serve and love God, he always works in *peace*, and usually *slowly*.[5] Why in peace? Because, as St. Ignatius explains it, the soul seeking to serve God is basically attuned to him and, while there may be things in such a soul that God wants changed, he does not want to create turmoil, to call into question the basic orientation—what we would call today the fundamental option—of the soul.

This rule, so simply stated, can be enormously helpful to the beginner. Let us take an example which is quite common in a country like the Philippines, where many families are poor. A seminarian comes to me with a dilemma: he wants to continue for the priesthood and yet his family is in financial need. Should he leave or should he stay? What really is God's will for him? Frequently I find it very helpful to ask him: "How do you feel about it when you are most at peace?—When you are at prayer and quiet (not emotional) and most open to whatever the Lord wants?" Very often he will reply: "At such times I always feel God is asking me to persevere and he will take care of my family. It is only when I am reflecting on it myself outside of prayer that doubts arise and I feel maybe God wants me to leave." In such a case I can say confidently to

---

[5]The idea that God works in peace is basic to the tradition of discernment. See, for example, St. Ignatius' *Spiritual Exercises*, "Rules for the Discernment of Spirits," rules 1, 2, and 5 of the first week, and rules 1 and 7 of the second week; pages 141-143 and 147-148 of the translation by Louis J. Puhl, S.J. (The Newman Press, 1960).

the seminarian that God's will for him is to persevere[6] and that he should not doubt this unless and until he feels God is speaking differently, precisely at those times when he is most at peace.

I said that God works not only in peace but *usually slowly*. This certainly is the pattern of Jesus' formation of the apostles, and it seems to be the lesson of the history of the Church. I am convinced that there are no shortcuts to holiness, despite the fact that men and women are always looking for a shortcut. The seed that springs up quickly does so because the ground is shallow and the nourishment is all going into the stalk and leaf instead of into the roots —and such plants quickly die, as Jesus says (Mk 4:5-6). Cursillos don't really aim to change men definitively overnight. Charismatic prayer does not effect instantaneous sanctity.[7] God chooses to work slowly, and we must have great patience, with him and with ourselves, on the road to holiness.

The one clear example of a sudden transformation might seem to be St. Paul, whose life was changed in an instant when he was stricken by a light from heaven as he journeyed to Damascus (Acts 9:1-8). But Paul himself tells us (Gal 1:16-20; Acts 22:9-16) that it took some time, including, apparently, a long retreat in Arabia's desert, for him to learn the Lord's will for him. In fact, Paul's full transformation from Saul to Paul took much longer still, as Romans, Chapter 7, makes painfully clear.

(3) A final rule for the beginner is this: Real growth

---

[6]The situation could be reversed, e.g., when prayerfully at peace, the seminarian feels he has no vocation, and doubts about his leaving arise only outside of prayer (when he begins to think about parting from all his seminarian friends). In this case, the sign would suggest at least the probability of a lay vocation.

[7]This is not to belittle the cursillo or the charismatic renewal, or similar movements. It is just a warning that we should not expect of them what they cannot give. Properly understood, the cursillo and the charismatic community underscore the need for gradual growth.

in knowledge of God and sensitivity to his will normally require a good spiritual director. We discussed this point briefly above in explaining the role of a director as a co-discerner. But it is important to make it a guiding principle of attunement to God that we must be open to hear him through his human instruments. Paul had to go to Ananias to learn God's message to him. Why did the Lord not tell Paul directly? He could do so, and in the lives of some few saints he apparently has done so. But in general the sacramental principle works in our lives: God works through human instruments, in forgiving, in consecrating—and in revealing his will. As St. Ignatius says, in the 13th rule for discernment of the First Week, the devil loves secrecy. Like a false lover, he will try to persuade the soul to keep its doubts and trials secret—because "no one will really understand," or because "I have to learn to stand on my own feet." How many times I have seen, in my own life and in the lives of those I direct, the wondrous way the Lord blesses openness! Anxiety is dispelled and peace descends and the road ahead becomes clearer because we have listened in faith to God speaking through another person.

It has been said that he who guides himself has a fool for a guide. This is not entirely true, since, as we have stressed earlier, the goal of good direction is the formation of mature and responsible Christians, who can properly discern the Lord's word to them. But it is undoubtedly true that he who listens *only* to himself has a fool for a hearer. As a matter of fact, such a person does not listen only to himself, but also, albeit unwittingly, to the evil spirit.

In this first part of the book, we have considered the "who" and the "what" of prayer. We have defined prayer as a personal encounter with God in love. We have explored the paradox that prayer is both irrelevant and supremely relevant to our daily lives and concerns. We have also noted some important basic guidelines for determining that we are truly hearing God. With this solid foundation we can safely and confidently proceed to a consideration of the "how" of prayer. We can ask about techniques of prayer, fully aware that the initiative is God's, and that most of the work must be done by him.

The How of Prayer

4

Are There Techniques of Prayer?

The past 15 years have been a time of unusual ferment in the Church, with radical change suddenly overtaking many stable institutions and practices. Formation in prayer has not been exempt from this ferment. For generations, beginners in prayer had been nurtured on point books and other aids to meditation. Seminarians learned to pray by gathering in the seminary chapel for a daily reading of a meditation, with appropriate pauses for them to reflect personally on what they had heard. Even the colloquies, or personal conversations with the Lord, which were supposed to conclude the time of prayer were often read aloud to the group or spelled out in a book. Mental prayer, as it was called, had a well-defined structure: preparatory acts, the reading of the text, personal reflection and the concluding colloquy. Learning to pray meant becoming familiar with this structure and letting it become second nature in one's life. The patterns which could sustain one for the next 50 years of active life were thus acquired.

Then, in the mid-1960's, things suddenly changed. The whole structured, point-book approach to prayer seemed much too rigid and impersonal in a spirit-led world. The fresh air which the great Pope John XXIII let into the Church seemed to topple the structures that had stood for so long. Prayer should be personal, spontaneous, unique to the moment. How could the Spirit of God be bound by the repetitive, mechanical structures of prayer which man devised? Who, after all, could *teach* another person how to pray, or pass judgment on the genuineness of the other's encounter with the Lord?

Many people involved in formation lost their self-confidence and virtually abandoned their formative role at this time. Given the drastic changes taking place, how could any man or woman (especially a child of Vatican I) presume to teach another how to encounter God? Father Henri Nouwen, in a classic chapter of *Intimacy* entitled "Depression in the Seminary," has discussed the overall effects, psychological and spiritual, of this collapse of confidence. It led to a situation in which leaders were unable or unwilling to lead, and in which followers gradually discovered that they were wandering alone in darkness. With respect to formation in prayer, it meant that no formation came to be considered the best formation—or at least the only one possible.

If this seems exaggerated, I well remember a situation which dramatizes the sudden and drastic shift in formation. As a graduate student at the University of Notre Dame in the late 1960's, I was an unofficial chaplain to the women religious in graduate studies. For most of the sisters, graduate studies were (like ordination for a Jesuit) the reward of a life well spent; they had already seen the darker side of 30. Thus our discussions often centered on the defects in our formation, and particularly the overly structured, mechanical approach to prayer from which we seemed to be struggling to free ourselves.

One sister, just out of the novitiate, was much younger than most. She was an active participant in our discussions, but it was only in private conversation with her one day that I realized how dated our hang-ups seemed to her. She said she could appreciate the difficulties the others were expressing, but she didn't think they realized how much things had already changed. They were concerned about a lack of freedom of spirit; her problem—and, she felt, that of her peers —was that nobody had given them any definite guidance on how to pray. They were subjected to a sink-or-swim approach to prayer: Throw the baby in the water and it will either learn to swim (to pray) or it will drown. What she felt was most lacking was any guidance in learning to swim in the sea of the Lord.

I was startled at the time, but in the years since I have shared this experience with many people of post-Vatican II vintage and have become convinced how accurately she represented their feelings. The sink-or-swim approach can perhaps, with grace, produce a few genuine pray-ers at an early age—but only at the cost of many tragic drownings!

Our story does not, of course, end there. Soon enough the rejection of classical method in prayer led to a search for new and better methods and techniques: a fascination with the Orient in its pure forms of yoga and Zen as well as its commercialized hybrids like transcendental meditation; a gradual institutionalizing of the structures of charismatic prayer; a search for gurus from whom one could acquire the key to unlock the inner realm. The implication was, in other words, that it was not method itself which was bad—but the *old* methods which were defective. There has been a return to method without a return to the traditional methods, among those who seek to encounter the Lord today.

It is in this context that we must ask about techniques of prayer. To ask whether there are such would have seemed peculiarly wrong-headed 15 years ago—of course there are! And 10 years ago the answer for many, spoken with equal conviction, would have been, "Of course not!" Now, perhaps, we are not so sure. We want techniques, but we fear the rigidity of established techniques. Deep down, perhaps, what we really want is a surefire technique, which is quick and painless and does not involve the labor and uncertainty of the past. If so, we are seeking for a shortcut to holiness, and we have already said that there is no such thing. In this sense there are no foolproof techniques of prayer.

Let us, however, not dismiss the whole question of technique or method so quickly. Our uncertainty today is healthy and reflects a genuine problem in prayer. How can we learn unless some man teaches us? (cf. Rom 10:14). And yet, how can we be taught without thereby "binding the Spirit" (cf. 2 Tim 2:9) and imposing our ways on God?

The last question raises a fundamental point, so let us begin from there. Since the Spirit is free to "breathe where he wills" (Jn 3:8) and to speak as and when he chooses, there clearly cannot be any techniques for making him speak. We cannot turn God on and off like a water faucet or an electric light. For this there are no techniques. So radical is our dependence on the good pleasure of the Lord that we cannot even *desire* to pray unless God draws us.[1] Even the beginnings are sheer gift. Hence no techniques of "meditation," be they yogic or transcendental or Ignatian, can ever guarantee an encounter with the Lord.

Granting this very important point, let us return to the first question above: How can we learn to pray unless some man teaches us? It might seem from the above paragraph that human teaching is of very little relevance here, that God speaks to whomever he wishes and whenever he chooses—and that is all we can say. To assert this, however,

---

[1]This is a very consoling and important point in these times of dryness known as the "dark night" or the "prayer of faith": even the desire to pray is a clear sign of God's presence, for without him we could not desire him.

is to overlook the apostolic and sacramental nature of the Church: God has chosen to work through men, and to embody his gift of grace in visible, structured signs. With respect to prayer he has willed that we learn through the teaching of other men and women. When I was young, I decided one day to read about John of the Cross. I was eager to learn to pray, and it seemed best to sit at the feet of an acknowledged master. But the more I read, the more troubled I became; it seemed that, if John was right, my whole intellectual and apostolic life as a Jesuit was wrong. Fortunately, before I ran off to be a hermit I spoke to my spiritual director. What he said wounded my pride, but it was just what I needed to hear: "Maybe you are not yet mature enough to read John properly and to understand him. Maybe you will just have to wait awhile before you can profit from his teaching." The advice was painful to accept, but I followed it—and have since repeated it to others more than once! But, to be more precise, just what is it that a good spiritual guide can teach us? In what sense are there communicable techniques and methods of prayer?

I believe there are two senses in which we *can* speak legitimately of techniques of prayer. In the first place, we can speak of techniques for coming to quiet, for bringing ourselves to that stillness in which the voice of God can be heard. Secondly, we can speak of techniques for positively disposing ourselves to encounter the Lord. For the Christian, of course, neither is possible—nothing good is possible —without the grace of God. But each of them does represent a way that we can and must cooperate with grace in opening ourselves to the advent of the Lord in our lives.

St. John of the Cross, with St. Teresa of Avila the Church's preeminent doctor of prayer, began his treatment of the topic with that purification of the soul which must precede transforming encounter with God. He distinguishes between the active and the passive purification which takes place: the active being what *we* can do to dispose ourselves for God and the passive being what *God* does to dispose us.[2] For John, the passive purification—what God does to purify us—is far more important, but he is by no means a quietist or passivist; for him, what we contribute, while secondary, is essential to growth. We cannot simply sit back and leave all to God. In prayer, for Teresa as for John, God helps those who do what they can to help themselves.

Suppose that I want to listen to a radio or TV program. I must get away from or block out other competing noises— this is coming to quiet—and I must turn on and tune in the radio or TV—this is positively disposing myself to hear. Neither will produce the sound if the station is not broadcasting, but both are necessary if I am to hear whatever is being broadcast. Let us now examine how each part of our radio analogy applies to techniques of prayer.

God, obviously, is the broadcaster, and our hearts and minds are the receiving sets. How do we go about getting away from or blocking out other competing noises? How, that is, do we come to quiet? The first point we can make is that coming to quiet is *essential* to prayer. That our analogy to radio or TV is applicable to prayer is clear from a famous passage in the First Book of Kings (19:11-13). The prophet Elijah has aroused the enmity of the evil queen, Jezebel. She threatens to kill him because of his prophesying. Frightened and discouraged, he goes "a day's journey into the wilderness" and lies down to die. But the angel of the Lord feeds him and leads him to Mt. Horeb to speak to the Lord. We are told that he stood upon the mountain waiting,

---

[2]See especially *The Ascent of Mount Carmel*, Book I, Chapter 13; pp. 152-153 of the translation by E. Allison Peers (Doubleday-Image paperback, 1958). John treats of the active purification in his first great work, *The Ascent of Mount Carmel*, and the passive purification in the second, *The Dark Night of the Soul*. Both are commentaries on the same poem—a classic of the Spanish language which begins "On a dark night, kindled in love with yearnings . . ."

And behold, the Lord passed by, and a great and strong wind rent the mountains, and broke in pieces the rocks before the Lord, but the Lord was not in the wind; and after the wind an earthquake, but the Lord was not in the earthquake; and after the earthquake a fire, but the Lord was not in the fire; and after the fire a still, small voice.

And the still, small voice was the voice of the Lord. Elijah heard the Lord's healing word to him, but only when he was able to hear that "still, small voice." God speaks in silences, and only those who are quiet of heart can hear what he says.

It is in coming to quiet that the techniques of yoga and Zen can be of help to the pray-er. They are essentially ancient methods for withdrawing from the distractions of ordinary life, and for coming to what the Buddha would call "The still center of the turning world."[3] Over the centuries yoga and Zen developed highly formalized traditions and rubrics, but at heart they seem to have been experiential— attempts by holy men of the East to share with their disciples methods which they had found helpful in coming to quiet.[4] They are not an end in themselves, nor are they a magical means to anything. But they are means which many have

---

[3]The phrase is used by a prominent contemporary Buddhist writer, Christmas Humphreys, in describing the ultimate contemplative goal of the Noble Eightfold Path of Buddhism (Christmas Humphreys, *Buddhism,* Pelican paperback, 1969, p. 117). T. S. Eliot uses a similar phrase ("the light is still/ at the still point of the turning world") in *Four Quartets* ("Burnt Norton," IV), and William Johnston, S.J., derives from Eliot the title of his "Reflections on Zen and Christian Mysticism": *The Still Point,* Perennial Library paperback (Harper and Row), 1970. For a fuller description of the Buddhist experience of this "still center," see Humphreys, *Concentration and Meditation,* Pelican paperback, 1973, pp. 158-161.

[4]This is not to say that this is *all* that yoga and Zen are intended to be. The fact that Christian prayer is an encounter with a personal God, whereas Hindu and Buddhist prayers generally are not seen as such, would give a very different coloring to yoga and Zen, as practiced by a Christian and as practiced by a Hindu or Buddhist.

found helpful in achieving a genuine quiet of heart. As such they can be as useful to the Christian as to the Buddhist. They are not, however, the only means to this end. In fact, when I discovered yoga myself, and attempted to practice some of its basic exercises, I realized that I had already learned, or worked out for myself, similar techniques. The preparatory acts in the old schema of meditation had a similar purpose when properly understood and practiced. One was told to take some moments to recall the scriptural theme of the day's prayer; to recall who God is and who I am, and what a wondrous thing it is that God should speak to me (the analogy of coming into the presence of a human king was often used); to "place oneself in the presence of God" in reverence and in humility. These steps, adapted to the circumstances of the individual pray-er, still form a very effective means for coming to attentive quiet.

Similarly, people often ask me whether walking is proper during prayer. St. Ignatius mentions various postures as helpful in prayer—sitting, kneeling, standing, lying prone or supine—but, significantly, does not mention walking. I believe the reason is because walking, or quietly strolling about, can be a very helpful means for coming to quiet and achieving attentive peace, but would be a distraction once we are at peace in the presence of the Lord. Notice how two friends strolling together often stop and face each other when they come to a point of deep sharing. Their strolling, as it were, creates the mood of encounter. Good classical music can also be a very effective instrument in this coming to quiet and achieving an attentive and concentrated spirit.

I suspect this also was the origin of ejaculations as a form of prayer. Like the Jesus prayer of orthodoxy or the mantra of Hinduism, the ejaculation was a short prayer form repeated over and over again. This repetition of the same formula, slowly and quietly, can be a great help in stilling the distracted spirit. But the subsequent stress on indulgences for saying ejaculations may have obscured the real value of these short prayers. If we become preoccupied with supernatural bookkeeping, then the *number* of such prayers said occupies our attention, rather than their value in bringing us to quiet before the Lord.

Even the repetitive structure of the rosary seems to be valuable to prayer in the same way. Used in such a manner, the *specific* content of the rosary prayers or ejaculations or the Jesus prayer would not be so important; rather they would be seen primarily as a help to achieving a prayerful spirit and a tranquil and attentive heart.

I have also found the divine office, or Prayer of Christians, helpful in achieving the same end. Often people ask me how to give more meaning to the office; they seem to find the familiar structure and repetitive phrasing a source of boredom or monotony, rather than a help to devotion. If, however, the office is seen primarily as a way of coming to quiet before the Lord—of being *reminded* of his love and providence at certain pivotal moments of the day, rather than as a source of *new* ideas about God and his place in our lives—then perhaps the repetition of familiar phrases can be seen in a new and more fruitful light.

The means I have suggested—ejaculations, the rosary, and especially the divine office—are already properly prayer since they entail a coming to quiet before, or in the presence of God.[5] Other simple practices, while not explicitly prayer in the same sense, can also help to bring us to quiet and open us to God. For example, psychologists suggest that we concentrate on our own bodies—first, let us say, on our right foot, gradually "thinking" our big toe into a relaxed state, and then our other toes in turn, then our instep, our ankle, our calf, our thigh, and so on until our

---

[5]St. Teresa calls this use of vocal prayers to come to quiet in the Lord's presence the prayer of recollection. She has some very helpful comments on it in *The Way of Perfection,* Chapter 29.

whole body is relaxed. I have tried this with various groups, and have been happily surprised at how helpful it can be. One interesting side benefit is that it often reveals to us where our real tension or disquiet is. People have said, "I am all relaxed, except for my mouth"—or ". . . except for a place on my forehead between my eyes." This says much about the source of our anxiety; once we realize it, we can begin to work in a concentrated, but peaceful, way on overcoming it.

Another exercise which I have discovered for myself, and have found very helpful, is the following: to get outside in a place where a panoramic view of nature confronts me, and where I can let my eyes wander over the entire scene (for example, a hillside overlooking a woods). I find it good just to let my gaze wander over the scene, without any concern for time and without any attempt to force concentration. Gradually one part of the woods catches my attention, and then one tree, and eventually one branch on the tree. My scattered thoughts come to focus on a single experience, and then dive deeper and deeper into that one reality (the universe in a blade of grass). Oftentimes the result is that my attention is absorbed by some small flower or leaf at my feet which I had not even noticed before— and I am at peace!

We have been discussing various techniques for coming to attentive quiet before the Lord. Not all of them are prayer proper—i.e., a personal encounter with God in love —but they are a normal prerequisite for prayer. The effort to come to quiet can often be the principal effort of the beginner. Today, especially, we live in a scattered and distracted world; it can be a major achievement just to come to peace. At the same time, it is important to realize that, for the Christian at least, this is only the preliminary step. As we grow and mature in prayer, we will be able to come to quiet more quickly and more easily. In fact, if we are faithful to prayer, we will find a natural drawing to quiet

as the state where we are most at home. This takes time, and
the beginner may have to exert long effort to mature in this
way—but it is important to remember that it is only the
beginning. The effort to come to quiet is not in itself prayer.
The time will come when the gazer must close his eyes,
when the background music must be turned off, when the
stroller must sit still and the pray-er of ejaculations must
keep silent—the time, that is, to "be still, and know that
I am God" (Ps 46:10).

5

The Active Purification of the Soul

In the last chapter we raised the question whether there are techniques of prayer, and we saw that there cannot be, in the sense of techniques for guaranteeing an encounter with the Lord. He is Lord, and his coming to us is sheer gift. We said, however, that we can speak of techniques with respect to prayer in two senses: techniques for coming to quiet, which we discussed in the preceding chapter, and techniques for positively disposing ourselves to encounter God. The two are not entirely distinct, and they do overlap; but the difference I have in mind is clearer if we recall the radio or TV analogy. We may not hear the radio because there is too much noise around us—and in this case we need to get the noisemakers to quiet down, or else get away ourselves to a quiet place. On the other hand, we may not hear the radio because it is not working properly, or because it is not turned on or not tuned in. In this case, it will not help us to be quiet, unless we also fix the radio, turn it on, tune it in. It is this latter repairing and tuning that we are concerned about when we ask, in this chapter, whether there are techniques for positively disposing ourselves to encounter God.

The radio analogy is a good one. Just as a broken radio set cannot pick up the broadcast, so too a broken soul cannot hear God. Sinful man must first be healed, "repaired," purified, before the voice of the Lord can truly penetrate his spirit. This is clear from the scripture and from the whole tradition of the Church. In a beautiful but ironic exchange with the scribes and Pharisees, Jesus says: "Those who are well have no need of a physician, but those who are sick," and he immediately goes on to apply this to himself: "I came not to call the righteous but sinners" (Mk 2:17, and the parallel verses in Matthew and Luke). The passage is ironic because Jesus really means that *all* of us are sick and he came for all. All of us have been poisoned by original sin. But the divine physician can only heal us if we are willing to acknowledge our illness and to seek healing.[1]

This need to be purified is difficult for men to accept in every age. Especially today, people want a religion of joy and fellowship and camaraderie—no hell, no pain, no penance. But the gospel knows nothing of such a painless faith. The grain of wheat must die before bringing forth a rich harvest. The hundredfold can be possessed only by those who leave everything to follow Jesus. In Baptism, the old man must be crucified, that he may rise to a new life in Christ.[2] It is not a popular way today, and it never has been, but it is the only way.

This is even clearer if we consider two of the works on prayer which the Church has recognized as perennial classics: *The Spiritual Exercises* of St. Ignatius Loyola and the *Ascent of Mount Carmel* of St. John of the Cross. Both Ignatius and John of the Cross were contemplatives of a

---

[1]See Jn 9:39-41, where Jesus, having healed the blind man, develops the same idea in terms of the metaphor of blindness.
[2]Jn 12:24; Lk 18:29-30; Rom 6:6.

high order, who drew on their own deep experience of the ways of God in writing about the interior life. It is striking, therefore, to see how strongly both of them stress the long process of purification which precedes true union with God.

At the very beginning of the *Spiritual Exercises,* St. Ignatius places this title: "Spiritual Exercises, which have as their purpose the conquest of self and the regulation of one's life in such a way that no decision is made under the influence of any inordinate attachment."[3] The language is striking—the very purpose of the Exercises is the conquest of self and the freeing of ourselves from any inordinate attachment which might color our decisions and distort our vision of the divine will. An eminently practical purpose, worthy of a practical man, but far from the contemplative grandeur we might expect. The reason, I think, is that these are exercises, things *we* can do to dispose ourselves for God. The contemplative experience is God's pure gift; the spiritual exercises which we undertake are, Ignatius says, ways "of preparing and disposing the soul to rid itself of all inordinate attachments, and, after their removal, of seeking and finding the will of God in the disposition of our life."[4] What Ignatius calls exercises are what we have called techniques for positively disposing ourselves to encounter God.

John of the Cross was a younger contemporary of Ignatius (he was born in 1542, while Ignatius died in 1556) who received his early education under Ignatius' Jesuits at Medina del Campo in Spain. John, however, was drawn to the contemplative life, and soon after his ordination in 1567 he joined with St. Teresa of Avila in the discalced Carmelite reform. At the time they met, John was 25 and Teresa was 52. Despite the disparity in their ages, and despite the fact that they were of remarkably different temperaments, John and Teresa became one of the greatest teams in the history

---

[3]Page 11, par. 21, in the translation by Louis J. Puhl, S.J.
[4]Page 1, par. 1, in the Puhl translation.

of spirituality. Both are doctors of the Church today, recommended to Christians precisely as masters of prayer.

It is striking, then, that John of the Cross, whose name has become virtually synonymous with Christian mysticism, should present a doctrine on the foundations of prayer very similar to that of Ignatius.[5] It is, in fact, from John that we have taken the title of this chapter: "The Active Purification of the Soul." We explained above (pages 60-61) that John distinguishes between the active and the passive purification of the soul. Active refers to what we must do to dispose ourselves to encounter God, whereas passive refers to what God does to purify us. The latter, for John, is much more important and is the subject matter of the *Dark Night of the Soul.* There are, in fact, two dark nights which John describes, that of the senses which "is common and comes to many (and) they are the beginners" and that of the soul or spirit, which "is the portion of very few (namely), those who are already practiced and proficient."[6] Although John here refers to those who experience the dark night of the senses of beginners, they are not really beginners in prayer. In Book I, Chapter I, in fact, John says this passive dark night begins when God begins to lead souls beyond the state of beginners; he says there that beginners are "those that meditate on the spiritual road,"[7] those who are engaged in the active purification of the soul described in the *Ascent of Mount Carmel.*

It is in this latter sense that we can properly speak of beginners in prayer. For reasons that will be clearer in the next chapter, they are those who meditate, whose prayer may properly be termed meditation. Meditation is, in fact,

---

[5]The same could be said, with equal validity, of the teaching of St. Teresa of Avila. See especially her *Way of Perfection,* which she wrote when her nuns asked her to teach them how to pray. See also the first three Mansions of the *Interior Castle.*

[6]Book I, Chapter VIII of the *Dark Night of the Soul;* p. 61 in the excellent translation of E. Allison Peers (Doubleday-Image, 1959).

[7]Page 37 in the Peers translation.

the way such beginners, during their time of prayer proper, may positively dispose themselves to encounter God. This, however, is not all that beginners can or must do to prepare themselves to meet the Lord. In addition to meditative prayer—which, as we will see in the next chapter, is a way of coming to know who *God* is and what he stands for— we need techniques to bring us to a deeper and more honest knowledge of ourselves, and to enable us, with the help of grace, to purify in ourselves whatever makes us unworthy of standing in God's presence. Let us consider these techniques now.

The basic principle of purification is that knowledge of self and knowledge of God go hand in hand. We cannot come to a deep knowledge of God without, at the same time, coming to a profound realization of who we ourselves really are.[8] This is painful. One of the most obvious results of sin in our lives is that we find it very difficult to face honestly who and what we really are. Adam, as soon as he had eaten the apple, began to make excuses for his action. The people of Israel, when confronted by the prophets with hard truths about themselves, invariably reacted by trying to silence the prophets. The same pattern is evident in the reaction of the scribes and Pharisees to John the Baptist, and then to Jesus, in the Gospels. When Jesus stripped away their masks and revealed what was really going on in their hearts, they could not face the truth themselves or stand to be revealed before others as they really were. Rather, they acted defensively and sought to destroy Jesus, "just as they had attacked the Baptist" (Lk 7:31-34). St. John puts it powerfully in his Gospel, in his comment on Jesus' dialogue with Nicodemus:

> And this is the judgement, that the light has come
> into the world, and men loved darkness rather

---

[8]St. Teresa has an excellent discussion of the continuing need of self-knowledge, no matter how advanced our state of prayer. See *The Interior Castle,* First Mansions, Chapter two.

than light, because their deeds were evil. For everyone who does evil hates the light, and does not come to the light, lest his deeds should be exposed (3:19-20).

This is true, not just of the scribes and Pharisees, but of all of us. Think how children react when accused of wrongdoing—or even when they lose a game. Their first instinct is to save face, to deny the wrong or to find excuses for the loss. It is the mark of a truly mature person to be able and willing to be seen as he really is—and how few mature people there are, even among adults! Most of us wear masks. We are concerned about how we *appear* to others; and we even attempt to fool ourselves about ourselves. We find it very hard to face the truth about who we really are—this is why psychiatrists and psychologists never lack for clients. Their role is to help people strip off the masks and to face and accept themselves as they really are.

Psychiatrists deal with abnormal situations, i.e., situations in which the failure to face reality has led to serious difficulties in functioning as a human being. As we said, however, not only abnormal people tend to wear masks. We all do. All the masters of Christian spirituality—beginning with the Lord Jesus himself—have stressed the need to strip away these masks if ever we are to encounter God. Self-knowledge (with self-acceptance) and knowledge of God go hand in hand. It is a painful process to come to see ourselves truly, but "the truth will make you free" (Jn 8:32).

For John of the Cross, man's desires are the root of his lack of freedom. The active purification (what we ourselves do) consists in recognizing and uprooting these desires. In fact, John's stress on freeing ourselves from all desire (the *nada*, or stress that everything human and natural is nothing) is what has made him appear austere and almost inhuman to most Christian pray-ers. Very few read him and many who do are frightened away. But we must keep in mind that by desires John means those purely natural de-

73

sires of man which, however good or indifferent they may be in themselves, have not been tamed by the overmastering Spirit of God's love. Moreover, we must keep in mind the purpose of John's doctrine of *nada* or nothingness. He is very much attuned to the modern philosophy of freedom; freedom *from* something is worthless unless it is freedom *for* something else. If we seek to uproot all merely natural desires, it is only in order that we may be truly free to love. In fact, we can only love truly when we are free of pride, ambition, lust, and other self-centered desires natural to sinful man. "When I'm not near the girl I love, I love the girl I'm near" is a clever and witty line from a modern song, but what it describes is not love at all. True love makes a man indifferent to all competing desires. The man who truly loves his wife, and has grown to maturity in that love (a rare enough phenomenon, admittedly), is free from the desire for other women. The same is true of the person who has come to a mature love of the Lord.

This singleness of heart was beautifully and forcefully brought home to me one day. A woman who was very happily married was sharing with me the wonder of a love that had grown over many years between her and her husband. She said: "You know, the strange thing is that I can always tell, at a party, when he has had enough to drink and it is time to go home. From across the room, he will always begin winking *at me!*" She said it with pride, and she knew how fortunate she was. Their relationship was such, even after many years together, that he only had eyes for her. His heart was single, and all competing desires were not annihilated, but swallowed up in the one great love of his life. For this man, as I happen to know, the love of God was equally real and total. Love of God and love of wife were not competing desires; rather, one was the path to the other. As Rosemary Haughton has said so beautifully, the married person comes to the love of God *through* the love of a spouse, while the celibate comes to the love of men through the love of God.[9] The problem is not too many loves, but the fact that our loves are in conflict, are eccentric, not centered and integrated. This is the root problem for every pray-er, whether married or celibate. We can have many loves in our lives, but only one center, one sun around which all our loves are satellites.

Coming to this freedom to love is, for most of us, a long and gradual process, and one that requires a great deal of help—grace—from the Lord. Perhaps John of the Cross (a great poet, a Spaniard, a 16th-century man) does not make clear enough for contemporary man the gradualness and the grace required. But his basic point is as valid today as in his own time—to be free *for* God, one must be free *from* all conflicting natural desires. Jesus said it long ago: "No man can serve two masters; for either he will hate the one and love the other, or he will be devoted to the one and despise the other. You cannot serve God and mammon (i.e., money)" (Mt 6:24; Lk 16:13). In Matthew's Gospel, this passage is followed by Jesus' beautiful command to be free from all worry and anxiety, like the birds of the air, like the lilies of the field. This is precisely the point John of the Cross is making—to be free to love is to be free from all desire, all anxiety.

St. Ignatius Loyola, a practical, methodical man of decision and action, sees his Exercises as intended to free us from any inordinate attachment, from any desire which blocks love and loving service. The means he proposes are meditative prayer on the life of the Lord Jesus, who is always our model of total freedom to love; the practice of penance; and the examination of conscience. We will speak more fully of meditative prayer in the next chapter. Let us now consider the ancillary means of penance and the examination of conscience.

Penance is not fashionable today. The Eucharistic fast

9"Marriage and Virginity: Two Ways to One End," in *The Gospel, Where It Hits Us,* pp. 1-20.

has practically disappeared. Penitential practices in seminaries and convents—such as the discipline, the hairshirt, the penance table at dinner—have become the stuff of legend, with which older religious awe (or regale) younger religious about the good (or bad) old days. In the time of Teresa and John and Ignatius, and for long thereafter, penance played a very prominent part in spirituality. It was often practiced to excess, and much of the change today is good. But all the saints have recognized that there is no genuine holiness, no solid spirituality, without penance. Ignatius, who was a child of his times and originally practiced much more severe penance than we would consider reasonable today, gives remarkably balanced guidelines for the proper use of penance.[10]

Ignatius is speaking of voluntary penance, that is, penance freely undertaken. The first thing to stress is that such penance is never an end in itself; God does not enjoy our suffering in itself, nor may we undertake it for its own sake. No. Penance is always a means to an end, and it must be chosen as any good means is chosen—insofar as it helps to achieve the end in view. Ignatius says the legitimate reasons for doing penance are: to make satisfaction for our sins; to help overcome our selfish inclinations (what John of the Cross calls our desires); and as a form of prayer, "to obtain some grace or gift that one earnestly desires." Since penance is a means, we should always be clear what our purpose is in doing it, and should choose that penance which is best suited to accomplish our purpose.

Penance as a means of making satisfaction for our sins, while not very fashionable today, is clear enough to anyone who has loved and has hurt the one loved. We *need* to make amends, to show by some visible sign our sorrow for wounding love. It is far from true that "love means never having to say you're sorry." Such a love, for fallible

---

[10]*The Spiritual Exercises,* #82-89 (pp. 37-39 in the Puhl translation).

human beings, would be not love but selfishness and superficiality. We see here the real difference between Peter and Judas. Both denied the Lord. Both failed, one might say, equally seriously. Both were filled with remorse. But Judas *could not say he was sorry,* could not face the Lord and seek forgiveness. There is no contrast in scripture so dramatic as that between Judas' going out alone and hanging himself and Peter's leaping from the boat and racing to shore to encounter again the Lord he had betrayed just a short time before (Jn 21).[11] It is no accident that Jesus, after breakfast, leads Peter away from the group and, by means of the triple questioning, celebrates with Peter the Church's first liturgy of reconciliation. The triple denial and now the triple affirmation of Peter's love—the symbolism of the parallel was not lost on Peter, nor on the early Church. Men's love, frail and fallible as it is, *does* mean having to say—by word and by action—that you are sorry for wounding love.

Penance as a means to overcome our selfish inclinations or desires has a long history, even among the pagan Stoics, and is based on sound psychological insight. It is the *agere contra* of ascetical tradition—act against the natural inclinations which you wish to correct. If the sapling is bent to the east, pull to the west to straighten its growth. If you tend to overindulge in food or drink, cut down consumption even to less than is legitimate; in this way, the will is strengthened and the unruly instincts are brought under control. Here again penance is clearly a means and must be proportionate to the end sought. I well recall speaking with a good sister, who felt the need of more penance in her life and asked what I would suggest. "How about cutting down somewhat on food?" I proposed. "But," she replied, "I hate to eat anyway." Clearly for her that was not a helpful penance! I suggested some penance in the area of reading,

---

[11]See also Lk 22:61-62, where Luke recounts that Peter immediately repented when the Lord turned and looked at him.

and this time hit the mark. "I love to read," she said. "In fact, I devour the newspaper first thing in the morning." So I suggested, not that she stop reading the paper (which was necessary to her work), but that she wait until later in the morning to read it. This would not interfere with her apostolic effectiveness, but it would be a very good training of the will and mastering of desire. She happily followed the suggestion, and found it of great profit.

Penance as a form of prayer is somewhat more unusual. We don't often think of penance in this way.[12] But I think Ignatius' view of penance as a form of prayer is deeply incarnational. Man is not an angel, he is an embodied spirit. His most spiritual acts need to be incarnated, enfleshed, sacramentalized. In this sense, his acts of bodily penance are an embodiment, a visible expression of his inner attitudes. They should be done for God, and not to impress men (see Mt 6:16-18; 9:14-25); but they are an important human form of prayer. I have found, in fact, that at times when my spirit finds prayer hardest, my body, by its acts, can often say what my heart cannot. The Lord truly hears and blesses such penitential prayer.[13]

The other means which Ignatius proposes for disposing ourselves to encounter God, for freeing ourselves of inordinate attachments, is the examination of conscience. This is, in fact, the very first topic of *The Spiritual Exercises*.[14] It

---

[12]In Mark 9:29, an ancient tradition has Jesus reply to the disciples' discouragement at their inability to drive out an unclean spirit by saying: "This kind can only be driven out by prayer *and fasting*." Other ancient manuscripts omit "and fasting," and many scripture scholars today believe it is a later addition to the text. But the idea of fasting (penance) as a form of prayer has solid scriptural grounding. See Acts 13:3 and 14:23; and also Isaiah 58 and Matthew 25:31-46, where the prevailing idea of fasting is purified and subordinated to fraternal love.

[13]Ignatius says, in the rules for discernment of spirits (#319: rule 6 of the first week), that doing some penance can be a very effective way to counter desolation in prayer. It must always, however, be seen as a means, and used insofar as it helps (see #89).

[14]Numbers 24-43; pp. 15-23 in Puhl's translation.

is a topic which he always advises the director to include in a retreat, no matter how poorly educated or how ill-disposed the retreatant.[15] Moreover, Ignatius is reported to have said that he would rather have his disciples miss their meditation than miss their examen—a surprising preference in the light of the fact that the examen is widely neglected today. What, then, is this technique which Ignatius valued so highly?

Again, it is not new to him, nor is it uniquely Christian. Even the great pagan Stoics saw value in such a practice. If we wish to overcome our faults, it is a great help to focus our attention upon them—to be aware of how and when we fail, and to note any progress we make in diminishing the frequency of failure. This leads to what Ignatius calls a general examination of conscience, a practice which the Church has incorporated into Compline or Night Prayer in the divine office. For the Christian, of course, the examination of conscience is not merely a sound psychological technique. It is also a channel of grace, both in the sense that we ask God to help us to see ourselves, our sinfulness, as he sees us, and also in the sense that it is a call for his healing power to work in our lives. Thus the stress is not merely, or even primarily, on our own efforts to overcome our failings. The work of healing is the Lord's and the examen is an opening of our hearts to his healing touch.

Another sound psychological principle of growth is divide and conquer. When we resolve to live a good life, we soon realize that our failings are many. In fact, the devil uses this realization to discourage beginners. We want instant holiness, and normally all genuine growth is slow, gradual and painstaking. We become frustrated as we realize how slow our progress is. In fact, as we grow we begin to discover failings in ourselves—pride, envy, timidity, laziness —which we were not even aware of before. How many

---

[15]See the Introductory Observations (for the director), #18-19 (pp. 7-9 in Puhl).

times I have begun a directed retreat with someone who, while good, sees the problems in his life as due to others' and not to his own faults. He is convinced he has been misjudged, persecuted, overlooked. Yet he gives himself generously to the retreat, and as the days pass he is overwhelmed by the realization that his faith has been weak indeed, and that he has been so preoccupied with other people's attitudes that he has drifted far from the fervor of his first love. John's strong words to the churches (Rev 2:4-5; 2:16; 3:1-3; 3:15-16) are heard spoken to him. He begins to see the great love of the Lord for him and the many hypocrisies in his own response of love. The danger now is the temptation of Judas. Confronted with our own many infidelities, we may be paralyzed and unable to act.

How can we avoid discouragement? By stressing faith, humility, patience with ourselves, and by realizing the profound truth that, even in our own interior lives, it is far better to light one small candle than to sit cursing the darkness. This is the idea of the divide and conquer principle—single out our failings and work on them one by one. Don't expect to change everything at once, but work and pray to change one thing at a time, beginning with those failings which most impede our growth. This is what Ignatius calls the particular examination of conscience, which he also recommends as a daily practice, especially for beginners. It is a review of how I have done during the day in the one specific area where my failures seem most to block the genuine encounter with God which I seek. The focusing on this area is a sound natural help to growth—having to face myself honestly once or twice a day will gradually make me conscious of my failings at the very time I am inclined to commit them. It is also a channel of grace in the same sense as the general examen; I expose to the Lord the precise area of my greatest weakness, and ask that his saving power be brought to bear especially there.

Both the particular and the general examen are time-tested techniques for what John calls the active purification of the soul, for positively disposing ourselves to encounter God. Perhaps now we can see why Ignatius would rather have beginners miss their meditation than their examen. He is convinced, of course, that both are necessary. But a prayer life without the healthy and humbling self-knowledge which the examen brings is very likely to be shallow and romantic and eventually harmful. It can lead to that false mysticism —a self-centered, "hearts and flowers" type of spirituality which forgets that the grain of wheat must die before bearing fruit—which has always been a danger in the history of the Church.

True knowledge of God always goes hand in hand with a painful self-knowledge. John of the Cross expresses it beautifully by means of the famous metaphor of the log of wood being transformed into fire.[16] As the wood burns, it becomes blackened, it cracks and steams, and all the knotholes and flaws are exposed. If the log could speak it would cry out: "My seeking to become fire was a mistake! I am now worse than when I started—black, ugly and flawed. I was better off before." The log is the soul and the fire is God. And the truth, of course, is that the log is not worse off than it was before. All the ugliness and defects were present before but they were concealed. The only way the log can become fire is to be revealed honestly and openly as what it is in itself. The process is painful but, contrary to appearances, it is the mark of real growth in union with God. That is why good souls who are making real progress often feel they are regressing and getting further from God.

I have not discussed the mechanics, the specific methods which might be employed in the particular and the general examen. There are various effective structures for the examen in different spiritual traditions. Moreover, several good articles have been written recently on the ques-

---

[16]*The Living Flame of Love,* Book I, #16 (in the first redaction; #19 in the second redaction).

tion.[17] There is, however, one further question which we should discuss. It is sometimes said that this approach to the interior life is too negative and too introspective. Are we not focusing too much on ourselves, and ultimately encouraging scrupulosity?

The question is a valid one. From my experience as a director in contemplative communities, I am convinced that the great danger of the contemplative life is confusing prayer with introspection. The contemplative comes to find God and is in danger of finding himself or herself instead. Self-analysis, and even self-knowledge, is not the goal of the interior life for a Christian; knowledge and love of God are the goal. If our focus is on digging deeper and deeper into ourselves, we will end in scrupulosity and not in genuine holiness. Yet, as we have stressed in this chapter, genuine self-knowledge is a necessary means to and concomitant of a true encounter with God in love.

A classic distinction from moral theology can help us strike the proper balance here: a sensitive conscience is a mark of holiness; a scrupulous conscience is a mark of sickness. The scrupulous conscience sees sin where there is no sin, constantly fears that it has not been forgiven past failings, goes over and over again the same ground of self-analysis. This is productive of anxiety and destructive of

---

[17]Especially helpful is "Consciousness Examen" by George Aschenbrenner, S.J. (*Review for Religious,* volume 31, #1, January, 1972, pp. 14 ff.) He presents the examen positively, as a time to review God's blessings and gifts to us, as well as our failings; to see the latter in the light of God's goodness and our response, and not merely in relation to law. The same approach is very helpful in the sacrament of Penance, which is the means, *par excellence,* to the active purification of the soul about which we have been speaking. Despite the fact that the sacrament of Penance has fallen on bad days recently, I personally believe that it is essential to any genuine growth in holiness in the Church. It must, of course, be approached in the spirit of this chapter—as a *means* to liberation and growth— and not as a mere laundry list of sins. (See Edward Farrell, *Prayer Is a Hunger,* Chapter Four, "Penance: Return of the Heart"; pp. 40 ff., Dimension Books, 1972.)

peace. As we saw in Chapter 3 (page 51), God always works *in peace* with those who are seeking to serve him.

The sensitive conscience, on the contrary, is one that becomes progressively more aware of smaller, *but genuine,* failings. This is a real sign of growth. The closer we come to the Light, the darker our own darkness appears by contrast. The prostitute who is actively plying her trade is unlikely to be bothered by, or even to notice, smaller failings like a tendency to gossip or a neglect of daily prayer. If, however, she gives up prostitution and seeks to reform her life, she is very likely to become conscious of many smaller faults which she has never adverted to before. This is not introspection or scrupulosity, although the devil will probably try to persuade her that it is. It is a sign of a growing sensitivity of conscience, a growing awareness of who she truly is, and if she perseveres peacefully, it will lead to a genuine knowledge of God.

What we seek, then, in the active purification of the soul, is a true knowledge of ourselves and a deeper sensitivity of conscience. It is by no means the whole of Christian spirituality, but it is an essential foundation for prayer. The other foundation is laid in our prayer life itself. It is to the laying of this second foundation that we now turn in our continuing exploration of the early stages of the road to God.

6

The Ways of Prayer
of Beginners

Thus far in this book, we have discussed what prayer is, how it may be said to be relevant, and irrelevant, to the life of man in the world, and what role is played by techniques—both of coming to quiet and of purification—in disposing the soul to encounter God. One major question remains: What does the beginner do when he actually comes to pray? If experiential knowledge and love of God are, as we have said they are, the goal of a life of prayer, where does one go, what does one do, to encounter the Lord?

In a sense, as we have seen, he doesn't go anywhere or do anything. The Lord comes to him unexpectedly and at a time not of man's choosing, as he came to Peter in a fishing boat, Matthew in a tax-collector's booth, Zaccheus in a tree, Paul on a journey. Man is, as C. S. Lewis expressed it beautifully in the title of his autobiography, "surprised by joy." There are no rules to govern such an event.

Still, we must do something. The first surprise encounter with the Lord is never a final, completely transforming revelation. As T. S. Eliot has put it, it is a drawing, a calling to explore, to inquire, to search. Such a call demands a response from man. The call may come dramatically as it did with Paul or it may come so imperceptibly that we cannot even say when it happened, as in the case of a person who has absorbed the faith right from childhood with the very air he breathed. However it happens, the time comes when we sense the Lord's call to know him, to become his friends. As I noted in the Introduction, this book is written for all those who, in one way or another, have heard this call, and now find themselves asking: What is our response?

In Chapters 4 and 5 we have discussed two of the essential preconditions of any authentic response to God's drawing: coming to attentive quiet, and cleansing our lives of anything which would block or hinder our capacity to return love for love. But how do we actually respond to the word the Lord speaks to us? What do we say or do in prayer? The answer to this question is the topic of the present chapter.

We can begin with an analogy to the deepest form of human love, the marital love of a man and a woman for each other. Such a love takes many years to mature. We sometimes speak of love at first sight, but in the strictest sense there is no such thing. There can be attraction at first sight—a boy and a girl can sense something in each other which draws them together and makes them sense that this relationship promises to be different from any other they have experienced. But real love demands knowledge; we cannot love what we do not know. And so the boy finds himself wanting to know all about the girl to whom he is drawn. If the girl responds, they spend endless hours in sharing with each other—their past, their hopes, their fears, their frustrations. They may even spend an evening alone together, and then, after the boy takes the girl home and returns to his own home, spend another hour on the telephone sharing what has happened in the half-hour since they parted. It is exasperating to their fathers, who pay the telephone bills, and appears silly to any onlookers who are not themselves suffering from the same disease. But it is not as foolish as it appears. We can only love what we know, and the boy and girl during courtship are seeking that mutual knowledge which alone grounds genuine love.

The same need is present in our prayer life, our love relationship with God. Genuine love of God also demands a time of courtship. Here, too, we can only love one whom we know. There is of course an important difference: God has known us before we were formed in our mother's womb (Jer 1:5). He knows our inmost being, better than we know ourselves. He "searches all hearts, and understands every plan and thought" (I Ch 28:9). But, while he knows us fully, we do not know him. And before we can fully respond to his love freely poured out in us, we must come to know him.

Thus the first stage of a genuine interior life is learning to know the Lord. We saw in Chapter 5 that both Ignatius and John of the Cross refer to the prayer of beginners as meditation.[1] Meditation means precisely this—taking time to learn who this God is whom we are drawn to love, what he stands for, what he values, what it would mean to be his friend. We can learn this from a consideration of creation, since nature, other persons and we ourselves are all signposts which point to their Maker, reflections which reveal the Artist who shaped them. Thus, every human being can come to know the Lord.[2] For the Christian, however, the primary revelation of the Father

---

[1]Chapter 5, pp. 65 and 69. Teresa of Avila also discusses meditation in Chapters 12 and 13 of her *Autobiography,* and in Chapter 19 of the *Way of Perfection.* See also Boase, *The Prayer of Faith,* Chapter 5.

[2]See Rom 1:19-20.

is Jesus Christ. Hence the scriptures, which were written that we, who have not known Jesus in the flesh, may believe in him, are the privileged way for Christians to come to know God in and through Jesus Christ.[3]

Meditation, then, is the use of our understanding to discover who God is—to learn to know him more fully in order that we may love him more deeply and follow him more faithfully. The principal sourcebook of Christian meditation is the scripture, in which God reveals himself to us. We may say that meditation is not properly prayer in the sense we have defined it (a personal encounter with God in love)—but, because love depends on knowledge, meditation on the scripture is an essential first step to genuine prayer. Thus it is the principal activity of beginners when they come to pray.

It is important to note that this "meditation" on the scripture may start long before we begin a formal life of prayer. In a good Christian home, the values of the Gospel and the person of Jesus Christ will be communicated in the very air the child breathes. In the Sunday liturgy—particularly in the new liturgy with its reading of the scripture over a three-year cycle, and its stress on the homily as an exposition of the scripture readings—that knowledge of God which grounds genuine love can be communicated gradually and very effectively. A good Christian schooling contributes much to the same end. Hence the "beginner" to whom this book is addressed may not really be a beginner. St. Augustine expressed this beautifully long ago, at the beginning of his *Confessions*. He confronts the mystery of knowledge and love, of the priority of knowing God over seeking ("imploring") him, and he concludes: "My faith, Lord, cries to Thee, the faith that Thou hast given me, that Thou hast inbreathed in me, through the humanity of Thy Son and by the ministry of Thy preacher."[4]

---

[3]See Chapter 3, pages 49-51.
[4]*Confessions*, I, 1 (trans. Frank Sheed, 1943), p. 3.

For some people, this diffuse sort of meditation may well suffice to ground a mature life of prayer. But in my experience, both as a pray-er and as a director of others, those who begin to be serious about a life of prayer normally need a deeper grounding in the knowledge of the Lord of Love, a more systematic searching of the scriptures, such as the meditation which occupies Augustine himself throughout much of the *Confessions*. For some who come to pray there has been very little of Christian formation. And for others, that which has been "inbreathed" into us during our formative years often needs to be made properly our own, and integrated into that coherent knowledge of the Lord of Love which Vatican I calls "the connection of these mysteries (of faith) with one another and with man's ultimate end."[5] Gradually, as we meditate, the bits and pieces of our knowledge of scripture and of the Lord become one seamless whole and our love takes on a sharper focus.

Meditation books have traditionally recommended a structure of prayer for beginners. While details may vary, it essentially involves three stages: the remote preparation, the immediate preparation and the actual meditation itself. Let us assume that we choose to make our meditation in the morning. This is often the best time, before our minds are filled with the concerns and distractions of the day. In this case, the remote preparation—reading over the scripture passage we are going to pray about, and consulting one of the commentaries to clarify the context and the basic message of the passage which we have chosen—would take place the evening before. This remote preparation, along with our daily spiritual reading, plays a very important role

---

[5]The First Vatican Council, Dogmatic Constitution *Dei Filius* on the Catholic Faith, Chapter IV. Quoted in *The Christian Faith in the Doctrinal Documents of the Catholic Church,* eds. J. Neuner, S.J., and J. Dupuis, S.J., volume I, p. 48.

in opening and sensitizing our minds to the things of God.[6] Without this remote preparation, we will not be doing what we can to open ourselves to God. We will be coming to prayer too casually, taking God for granted. And it is unlikely that we will hear his word in this way.

The immediate preparation for prayer is what we do when we are ready to begin to pray. St. Ignatius recommends that we stand back from the place where we are going to pray, and take a moment to recall the passage or theme we are to pray about, and then recall what a wondrous thing it is that we seek to do. I have found a short prayer like the following very helpful: "Lord, I realize that you are truly present and anxious to teach me to pray. You care more for me than I care for myself. Help me to realize the wonder of your speaking to me, and to respond as generously as possible." The purpose of this short prayer is that I may come before the Lord reverently and attentively, as his holiness demands.

The remote and immediate preparations for prayer are very important, especially for beginners. The form they take may vary, of course. Perhaps the best way for the beginner is to start with some such format as I have described. Then, with experience, one can adapt it to one's own temperament and needs. The goal is to come to prayer prepared to hear the Lord, and reverently attentive to his word. To paraphrase St. Teresa, good preparation is whatever most helps us to pray well—whatever most moves us to love God.[7]

---

[6]I have found it important to stress to beginners that good spiritual reading is that which moves the will and not merely the understanding. The purpose of spiritual reading is to inspire us to act—to seek the Lord and commit ourselves to his service. Thus, good biographies of saints, and of great contemporary men and women of God, are excellent spiritual reading.

[7]*Interior Castle,* Fourth Mansions, Chapter 1: "The important thing is not to think much but to love much; do, then, whatever most arouses you to love." As we noted above (p. 63), in speaking of techniques for coming to quiet, the same flexibility should guide our choice of a place and a posture for prayer.

The third stage of the traditional schema of prayer is the actual prayer itself. This is what we have called meditation, and have described as the use of our understanding to come to know God more fully, in order that we may love him more ardently and follow him more faithfully. Actually, in the history of spirituality there has never been any one terminology universally accepted by all authors on prayer. Most use the word "meditation" more or less as we have used it above. Whatever the words chosen, the same essential points about the beginnings of prayer are found in all the Christian masters of prayer. But I have found it helpful to make a distinction here, between meditation and contemplation.[8] The basis of the distinction is this: Man is endowed with an understanding or reasoning faculty and with an imagination, and both faculties can be employed in coming to know someone or something better. Reasoning is more logical, more abstract; it considers causes and draws conclusions, often step by step. Imagination is more concrete, more specific; it sees a single event or situation in its concrete totality. Reason sees the logical links between events or actions ("The guitar is off-key; it must need tuning"), whereas imagination enters into, gets the feel of an actual experience ("What a strange feeling of desolation I get when I hear that guitar playing off-key!").

As we said, all of us are endowed with faculties both of reasoning and of imagination, and both faculties help us to know reality in different, but complementary, ways.

---

[8]The distinction between meditation and contemplation which follows is implicit in St. Ignatius' use of the words in *The Spiritual Exercises*. John of the Cross and Teresa of Avila tend to use the word meditation to cover both activities, because they use the word contemplation to describe a later stage of prayer in which God takes over and we are more passive or receptive. Authors have tried to clarify the situation by distinguishing between acquired contemplation (the beginner's type which we are discussing) and infused contemplation (the more advanced stage of prayer where God takes over more and more). We will say a word about infused contemplation in the Epilogue.

It often happens, though, that one faculty is dominant in a given person. Artists are often said to be more imaginative, and scientists to be more rational—although Bach or Mozart is much more "rational" than Brahms or Beethoven, and a creative scientist like Pasteur or Einstein must possess a strong imaginative faculty. Women are probably more imaginative, as a whole, than men, who tend to be more logical. I have learned that Filipinos—and perhaps Southeast Asians in general—are generally far more imaginative than their more analytical American or Chinese friends. The important point here is that men and women, not only groups but individuals, vary greatly in the mix of reasoning and imagination which they bring to the interpretation of their experience.

This is an important insight for beginners in prayer. We can come to know the Lord via our reasoning or via our imagination, or, more likely, via a very personal blend of the two. This is the basis of the distinction I have suggested between meditation and contemplation. Meditation is the use of the understanding, the reasoning faculty, to come to know God's revelation better, whereas contemplation is the use of the imagination to achieve the same end. Since both are good techniques for coming to know the Lord, and since some people will find one more helpful and some the other, let us discuss each more fully.

We can begin with meditation. And since, as we have said, the primary source of our knowledge of the Lord is scripture, let us take a passage from the Gospel of St. John as an illustrative example.[9] A very beautiful passage is the story of the Samaritan woman at the well in John 4. Jesus has been journeying through Samaria, the region between Galilee and Judea, and has sat down to rest beside Jacob's well. The disciples have gone into the nearby city of Sychar

---

[9]It is very helpful to choose as the subject of our meditation or contemplation the gospel passage from the liturgy of the day. In this way, the liturgy is enriched and made deeper by the reflections of our time of private prayer.

to buy food, so Jesus is alone at the well. A woman of the neighborhood comes to draw water at the well, and Jesus asks her for a drink. She is surprised that he would speak to a strange woman in public, especially since the Jews and the Samaritans were enemies. She expresses her puzzlement at his request, and Jesus replies by referring to the far better water which he could give her. This leads into the famous dialogue about the water of eternal life—a dialogue which results in the conversion of the woman and of many of her townmates. It is a very human passage, and one which brings out the simplicity of the woman and the gentleness of Jesus. Let us see how we would meditate on the incident.

Recall that meditation means using our reasoning to come to know God better. Here it would mean reflecting on the behavior of Jesus in this very concrete situation, and on the words he speaks to the woman, to discover more of God's ways with men. Why does Jesus speak to a strange woman, particularly to one who has had five husbands and is now living with a man not her husband, and who must have had a rather low standing in her town? What does this say about the way God judges people, as contrasted with the judgments of men? What implications does this have for the way I should deal with people if I am truly to follow Christ? Again what does Jesus mean by living water?[10] The woman misunderstands him. She thinks he has a secret source of natural water, but he very patiently uses her misunderstanding to teach her about the water of the Spirit. How deeply do I feel the desire for the living water of the Spirit? What in my life corresponds

---

[10]This is an instance where a good commentary—for example *The New Testament Reading Guide* series, Barclay or Peale, can be a great help in preparing for our prayer. "Living water" meant water that was flowing, as from a spring, which was very valuable in a semidesert country like Palestine, where stagnant water was dangerous and flowing water was scarce. Jesus uses flowing, life-giving water as a symbol for the inner "water" which gives life to our souls.

to the five and a half husbands of the Samaritan woman—
i.e., what blocks me from truly encountering Christ in my
life? How has the Lord used that very obstacle to reach
out to me? It is often said that we become most aware of
God when we are weakest and most aware of our sinfulness.[11] But not all sinners hear God's voice. What is there
about the Samaritan woman's attitudes which makes her
very sinfulness the basis for her encounter with Jesus?

The incident in John 4 is a rich and beautiful source
of meditative prayer, and our reflections above have only
scratched the surface of its treasure for the pray-er. But
perhaps we have said enough to make clear what meditation is: a reflective searching of the scriptures to discover
what God reveals of himself in the person of Jesus, and to
learn by analogy how he is speaking in the events of one's
own life. As Jesus tells Thomas, "I am the way, and the
truth, and the life; no one comes to the Father, but by me.
If you had known me you would have known my Father
also . . ." (Jn 14:6-7). Philip still does not understand,
and he says, "Lord, show us the Father, and we shall
be satisfied." But Jesus insists that "He who has seen me
has seen the Father" (14:9). This is the very heart of the
Christian faith: "No one has ever seen God: the only Son,
who is in the bosom of the Father, he has made him
known" (Jn 1:18). Jesus is *the* revelation of the Father for
men of flesh and blood. It is by studying his life—his
values, his attitudes, his ways of dealing with men—that
we learn who God is for us.[12]

In meditation, however, we reflect not merely on the
historical life of Jesus and the experience of the evangelists
and apostles. We also reflect on how God reveals himself
in our lives today. Jesus is the "firstborn of many breth-

---

[11]St. John of the Cross, in the *Spiritual Canticle* (stanza IV,
Exposition), says that we *first* encounter God in our sinfulness, and
only then in the goodness of creatures, and only lastly in himself.

[12]See also I Jn 4:9-15; Heb 1:3; I Pt 2:21; Rom 8:29; 2 Cor
4:4-6.

ren," and we are called to "have this mind among you, which is yours in Christ Jesus," to "put on the Lord Jesus Christ."[13] Thus meditation is not merely a reflective historical study of a past figure—no matter how important we may consider that historical figure to be. It is an attempt to discover, by means of the life and teaching of Jesus, how God is revealing himself through Christ in the events of our life today. Some of the questions we raised in our consideration of the Samaritan woman bring out this link between Jesus' early life and our search for God today.

As we have described it, meditation is the use of our reasoning powers. We said earlier that there is another, equally valid, way to come to know the Lord: contemplation. Contemplation is more imaginative, and is often helpful for those who find difficult the type of analytic reasoning we have described as meditation. The story of the Samaritan woman can be useful here, since it lends itself as easily to contemplation as to meditation. Let us contrast the two approaches by seeing what it would mean to contemplate the incident at the well.

Contemplation involves imaginatively entering into the incident we are considering—being present at the event, seeing it happen as if we were actually participants ourselves. This is a much easier task for children of a visual culture such as ours. Movies and TV draw us into an event, a story, in a way which the printed word cannot often duplicate.[14] In fact, I have found it very helpful to explain contemplation by likening it to our experience of a movie. Why is it that we weep at a tragic movie? Surely not because a piece of film is running through a projector, or because certain shadows are appearing on a screen! This is what is actually happening at the time, but there is

---

[13]Rom 8:29; Rom 13:14; Phil 2:5.

[14]It is true that a skilled storyteller, whether live or in print, has always been one who can totally involve his hearers in the story. But even news events have an immediacy, an emotional impact on TV which they never achieve on the front page of a newspaper.

nothing to cry about in that. Why, then, do we cry? Because we ourselves have become imaginatively involved in the story: we relive it in some way ourselves. We make our own the attitudes and feelings of the actors with whom we identify. We know how they feel because we feel and experience with them. We come to experience a long-lasting sense of kinship with characters from our favorite movies. Somehow they become part of our lives.

Contemplation is like this. We bring our human powers of imagination to our prayer, and we seek to relive, not some movie, but the life of the Lord Jesus. In our example, we seek to be present at the well when Jesus meets the woman. Perhaps we are sitting beside him as she comes walking along the road. We notice his face (he is "weary"). We see what a woman looks like who has had five and a half husbands, and who is tired of having to come to the well day after day. We feel the heat of the noonday sun in this semitropical land. We notice the shape of the stones in this ancient well, believed by tradition to date back more than a thousand years to Jacob. And then Jesus speaks to this strange woman. We hear his words, note the tone of his voice, observe the surprised look on the face of the woman. We listen, and look, as their dialogue unfolds—and we imagine how we would have reacted had we been in the woman's place. Perhaps we share her puzzlement at Jesus' reference to living water. Perhaps we find ourselves involved in the conversation, asking the Lord our own questions about eternal life, asking the woman what the Lord really said to her. She tells the people of Sychar that he told her "everything I have ever done"—which goes far beyond the conversation actually recorded in the Gospel. What would it mean to meet someone who tells *us* everything we have ever done? We may even, in our contemplation, find ourselves remaining at the well with Jesus, when the woman hurries off to town to tell the people—and we may learn by experience what it means to have him tell *us* everything we have ever done.

95

Like meditation, contemplation is not merely an imaginative reliving of the past. In experiencing with the Lord the concrete situations of his life, we come to discover how he is living and working in our lives. We too meet him sitting beside a well. We also recognize him in the breaking of the bread (Lk 24:35), and our imaginative reliving of the Gospel event gives way to our own encounter with the Lord. This element of personal encounter, of personal involvement, is what makes both meditation and contemplation different from the knowledge that the theologian or the historian, as such, might have of the same Gospel event. This *personal* knowledge is what makes meditation and contemplation properly prayer—i.e., part of the whole process by which we encounter God in love.

That is why the traditional manuals of prayer recommend that, right from the beginning, we end our prayer with a colloquy or conversation with the Lord. When we begin, the colloquy will be somewhat awkward and stilted, like a conversation with a stranger. But as we come to know God better, the colloquy will become more spontaneous and natural. Gradually the colloquy will become the substance of our prayer, as knowledge gives way to love. Then there will be less and less need for meditation or contemplation. Our primary need will be to be with the Lord, whom we have come to know and love—and that, as we have said, is the essence of prayer.

This makes clear the first important warning we must give concerning meditation and contemplation. They are the beginnings of a good prayer life, but reasoning and imagining are not ends in themselves. Prayer is not simply a lifetime process of understanding the Gospel and making applications to our lives. Nor is it a lifetime of imaginative involvement in the events of Christ's life. Too much stress on speculation and analysis would lead to an abstract and sterile concern with the "logic" of the Gospel. Too much stress on the imagination would lead to a false visionary kind of spirituality, which spent its time discovering what color cloak Jesus was wearing at the well, or how old the woman was. Both would wrap us up too much in ourselves and our own thoughts, and not open us enough to the transforming of God's word in our lives.

Another caution: fruitful meditation or contemplation is an art, and thus is not so much taught as it is learned by experience. Although we use our own faculties of reasoning and imagination, the knowledge we seek is ultimately God's gift. We should be willing to experiment with the approaches I have described, and to discover what is most suited to our own temperament and to the gospel passage we are praying over. Some passages (such as Jesus' discussion with the Pharisees about divorce or the beatitudes) are much more suited to meditation. Other passages (such as the raising of Lazarus or the annunciation) are ideally suited to contemplation. Many passages, such as the woman at the well, can be fruitfully prayed over in either way. These latter passages can be very helpful in learning which approach is more suited to your own temperament and needs.

Too often in the past, meditation has been presented as the *only* way for beginners. As a result, many people have found prayer extremely difficult, and have felt they were unable to meditate. Perhaps the reason why contemplation was avoided is because we thought of the imagination as too physical, too carnal—and too likely to lead us into temptation. But the imagination is an integral part of man, and many of the great pray-ers have been richly imaginative people. Grace builds on nature: it does not destroy it. What we must learn to do is to channel and discipline or imagination and our other faculties, not to kill them. If you tame a wild and spirited horse, you have something of great value. If you tame a timid horse you don't have much. If you kill a spirited horse, you have nothing but a carcass. This is why the active purification of the soul—which, along with the techniques for coming to quiet, is the taming of the wild horse in each of us—must always be employed only insofar as it contributes to our experience in prayer. Dispositive techniques are, as we have stressed before, means to an end. The end or goal is to encounter God and to respond authentically to his love.

Similarly, contemplation and meditation are means to an end. They are ways of coming to know the Lord in order that we may truly love him—not merely in word but in action. As such they will not normally continue throughout a whole life of prayer, just as courtship will not normally continue throughout the whole of married life. To put it more accurately, while the element of coming to know the Lord will continue in some way throughout life —just as a loving husband and wife never know each other "inside out" and are always discovering more about the mystery of each other—still it will later cease to play the dominant role it plays in the courtship period. We will say a word about what happens later in the Epilogue to this book; it takes us beyond this introduction to prayer. What is important here, however, is to realize that prayer is life. Like all life, it changes, it evolves.

There is evolution even within what we may call the beginner's state of prayer. There may be an initial infatuation with the Lord, corresponding to what, in human relations, we call love at first sight. As we seek to learn, by meditation and/or contemplation, who this mysterious person is to whom we are drawn, infatuation or emotional attraction gives way to a more sober knowledge of the Lord. He is *not* what our feelings would like him to be. Human lovers discover that the one they love is flawed and imperfect, and is very different from their romantic image. God is not flawed and imperfect, but he is different from our expectations. Every pray-er must learn, as the apostles did, that God is a very different savior from what they naturally expect. The sons of Zebedee sought glory and he offered them the cross.[15] Peter wanted to remain on Tabor,

---

[15]Mt 20:20-23.

but Jesus led him to Calvary.[16] At the very end of his earthly sojourning among them, they expected a political revolution to liberate Israel, but Jesus ascended to the right hand of the Father and left them, for a time, alone.[17] The God they learned to love was far different from the God they wanted to love! So it must be with us.

Coming to know the Lord is different for another reason also: He does not speak as men speak, with a voice we can hear with our ears. We do not look into his face as a boy and a girl courting can look into each other's faces. For this reason, beginners find meditation or contemplation laborious. Despite their sincere efforts, their attention span is short in seeking to know an invisible God. How often, in retreats, I have proposed to beginners a chapter, such as John 4, which is rich in insight. After an hour they return to say they finished that chapter in 10 minutes—and did not know what to do next! To dig deeper is laborious for beginners, and often seems boring.

The first time I had this experience, in a lay retreat in Syracuse, New York, I felt perhaps I was expecting too much of laymen—or perhaps that the style of prayer I was proposing was too much geared to religious. When the same problem recurred with sister-novices in the U.S., and with seminarians in the Philippines, I began to realize that the problem was a normal one for beginners. When these same people, as I had the chance to work longer with them, began to discover the riches of the scriptures and the God who is there revealing himself, it became clearer and clearer to me that this is a normal problem, and should not cause us discouragement. If we persevere, patiently and peacefully returning to our prayer whenever we become aware of being distracted, our perseverance will ultimately bear fruit. The time will come when it becomes easy and joyous to pray, and when the insights of our meditation and contemplation flow smoothly and almost

---

[16]Mk 9:4-9.
[17]Acts 1:6-9.

spontaneously. The riches of the scriptures will flow easily from the pages of the Gospels. There will be a new depth to our experience which makes prayer a joy. The same chapter which, in the beginning, was exhausted in 10 minutes, will provide more fruitful insights than we can digest in a day. We begin to see links between various gospel incidents. The Gospels become, not a series of isolated events touching diverse themes, but a portrait of a whole and very real person, Jesus Christ. We begin to discover, in him, the face of God for us.

When will this happen, and what does it mean? Each of us is unique, of course, and our experiences vary with our needs and with God's designs for us. But this new ease and joy in meditating will often come within the first year or two of a faithful and persevering life of prayer. It means that we are coming to be at home with the Lord, and that he is responding to our fidelity by guiding and deepening our thoughts. It will seem to us, at this point, that we have truly learned how to pray—that now, in fact, we have mastered the secret of the interior life and are well on our way to holiness. The truth, however, is that "no eye has seen, nor ear heard, nor the heart of man conceived, what God has prepared for those who love him."[18] We are only beginning to discover what the Spirit has to teach us of God—but it is a very good beginning.

---

[18]I Cor 2:9; cf. Is 64:4.

Epilogue:

Prayer Beyond the Beginnings

For some years I have taught a course on apostolic prayer. In one class, not many years ago, there was a sister who belonged to a contemplative community. We became friends, and I was privileged to become her director as well. One day, toward the end of the course, when we were discussing some of the points I had made in class, she said: "I found your lectures very helpful, but I wish you had said more about the *goal* of the interior life—where it is all leading, what the end result will be." I was puzzled and challenged by her comment, and we discussed it several times thereafter. In one sense, I felt I could not say any more about the goal than had already been said; all the saints, including John of the Cross, become strangely inarticulate when they come to describe the state of union with God which is the threshold to eternity.[1] How could I say anything when they were reduced to silence?

In another sense, I knew her question was valid and needed an answer. Knowing the goal of our journey is an

---

[1] See John of the Cross, *Living Flame of Love*, Stanza IV, par. 17.

essential condition of discernment: only if we know where we are going can we be confident we are on the right road. My attempts to formulate that answer—for myself, at least —have proven very fruitful to my own life and to my work as a spiritual director. What can *not* be described, I believe, is the *experience* of God which he gives to those whom he has wedded to himself. St. Paul acknowledged this when he sought to justify his mission by saying that he had once "been caught up into paradise"; he says of his experience that he "heard things that cannot be told, which man may not utter" (2 Cor 12:3-4). Earlier in the same letter (9:15) he concludes an appeal for support for the needy churches by contrasting the donations of the Corinthians with the incomparably greater gifts of God to them: "Thanks be to God for his *inexpressible* gift," which is the surpassing grace of God in them. The fullness of the experience of God is beyond words.

What can be expressed, however, is what the experience of God is *not*—and also what the manifest fruits of this gift should be in the here and now. In Chapter 6, I quoted a passage from St. Teresa's *Interior Castle* which has long been a favorite of mine: "The important thing is not to think much but to love much: do, then, whatever most arouses you to love." Teresa then goes on to clarify what precisely this love is, which we seek:

> Perhaps we do not know what love is: it would not surprise me a great deal to learn this, for love consists, not in the extent of our happiness, but in the firmness of our determination to try to please God in everything, and to endeavor, in all possible ways, not to offend Him, and to pray Him ever to advance the honor and glory of His Son and the growth of the Catholic Church.[2]

---

[2]The *Interior Castle,* Fourth Mansions, Chapter 1 (vol. 2, p. 233 in the Peers edition).

To love in this way—unselfishly, courageously and with a genuine passion for God's will "on earth and in heaven"—is the real goal of our life of prayer. St. Paul spells it out when he enumerates the fruit of the Spirit: love, joy, peace, patience, kindness, goodness, faithfulness, gentleness, and self-control.[3] These are the manifest fruits of a genuine prayer life. If we are growing in these, we are on the right road. To possess them perfectly, by the working of the Holy Spirit in us, is the goal of our prayer. The experience of God is not measured or validated by visions, ecstasies, magnificent insights or floods of tears. These phenomena may have their place for the edification of the Church and the encouragement of the pray-er, but they are not necessary to genuine holiness. In fact they are not even infallibly from God: their genuineness must be tested by the fruits of the Spirit we mentioned above. An ecstatic or a visionary who lacked deep peace and joy, real gentleness and self-control in his or her dealings with others, would make any good director very suspicious!

In this context, it might be helpful to say a word about *infused* contemplation, which we described briefly in a footnote to Chapter 6 (page 90). Recall first that we spoke in the Introduction of those spontaneous moments of prayer when, indeliberately as it were, we are aware of God's presence to us. Such moments may occur, even in the life of a beginner in prayer—in fact, even in the life of someone who would not consider himself a pray-er at all. As we stressed throughout the book, these encounters—these personal encounters with God in love—are the very essence of prayer at every stage of our development. All our talk of techniques, of meditation and (imaginative) contemplation, of coming to quiet and penance and the examen, was based on the conviction that these are the ways we *normally* can learn to respond to God *habitually*—to open ourselves to an *abiding* experience of his presence in our lives.

---

[3]Gal 5:22-23.

We might say that those occasional, indeliberate moments of contact with the Lord of Love which mark the early stages of a life of prayer are precisely God's way of drawing us to a deeper, because habitual, experience of his presence.

Put in this way, the whole point of Part II of this book has been to ask how we can best *respond* to God's initial drawing. "No one can come to me," Jesus says, "unless the Father who sent me draws him" (Jn 6:44).[4] Our efforts are vain unless God first comes to us. But if and when he comes, how do we respond so that his gracious initiative can bear full fruit in our lives? This is the principal question we have sought to answer in this book.

Now, as we respond to God in the dialogue of love which is our life of prayer and service, the time may come when God takes over more and more—when, in terms of our analogy of dialogue, we do less and less of the talking and God does more and more. We become passive (to use the term of the saints); we become more and more like the clay in the hand of the potter (Jer 18:6) to be shaped and molded by him. From the very beginning, God's grace is essential to any prayer, to any response of ours; but the time *may*[5] come when he not only gives us the grace to seek him, but himself does the work in us. This is what is known as infused contemplation, where, according to the theologians, not only is God's grace at work, but our very

---

[4] See also Jn 3:27; 6:65; 15:16; 17:9. Along with the correlative idea that "no one comes to the Father except through me" (Jn 14:6), this total dependence on God's drawing is a dominant theme of Jesus' preaching in John.

[5] I say "may" here because this passivity is a special and rather advanced experience in the interior life. John of the Cross, the master of higher stages of prayer, insists that it is sheerly gratuitous and that it may not be the experience of all—or even most—faithful pray-ers. For myself, I suspect that it is the normal terminus of a real life of prayer—but it is certainly a sheer gift of God, to which we have no right, and (barring a miracle of grace) it would come only after years of a more active response by the pray-er to God's word.

way of knowing him transcends our human powers of knowing and loving. Because our natural faculties are suspended, it is a "dark night," a "cloud of unknowing."

This discussion of infused contemplation may seem obscure and confusing to a beginner in prayer. If so, it is because this is not yet a part of his own experience. I mention it here, however, to give some faint outline of the road ahead in the life of prayer. Another, and more important, reason is to stress that the goal of *all* good prayer, no matter how elementary or how advanced it may be, is to transform our lives, to deepen and strengthen our love of God in action. Whatever our stage of interior growth may be, the growth in the fruits of the Spirit is the only touchstone of genuine prayer.

This knowledge of the goal of our prayers can help us to understand the way God normally leads us. We said that the way of beginners is usually meditation or contemplation, whereby they come to know who God is—to acquire that knowledge which is the necessary basis of genuine love. Toward the end of the last chapter, we said that the first breakthrough in our life of prayer is when our meditation or contemplation becomes easy and joyous. When we find much fruit in just a few verses of scripture, and when the Lord Jesus begins to be a real person for us. This breakthrough, which may come after a year or two of a serious life of prayer, may usher in a period lasting, with ups and downs, for several years. As I said, we are tempted to think we have truly grown: God is near and dear to us, practicing virtue is easy, and no sacrifice seems too costly if it is for him. We feel quite holy!

For example, at this time, failings in us which have been particularly deep-rooted—envy, irritability, a strong and unruly imagination—may suddenly disappear. We feel that we have finally mastered the dark side of ourselves, and are free of these faults forever. The real situation is quite different. It is not that we have grown so much but that God is spoiling us—in order to win us to himself.

The image I often use is that of a father and his year-old child. The baby has learned how to crawl all about the house. He has become a very skilled crawler. Then one day the father decides to carry the baby for a walk. As they walk out the door and down the street, the baby is very excited. Up to now his whole world has been knees and ankles and the bottoms of tables. Suddenly he sees things from his father's shoulder—and moves with the speed of his father's feet. If you have noticed a baby taken for a walk, you have seen that the baby usually thinks *he* is really accomplishing something himself. He kicks and pushes in his father's arms as if his feet were doing the work. When they return home, and Papa puts baby down on the floor again, the baby is frustrated. Left to himself, he can only crawl. It is not merely that the baby is right back where he started. Before the walk, crawling was all he knew and he was contented with it. Now he knows something better is possible, and crawling is no longer enough to satisfy him. He is, in a sense, worse off than he was before he discovered what fun walking can be.

It is like this in the early stages of our life of prayer. God is the father, and we are the baby. When we begin to make progress, it is not because we have learned to walk but because God is carrying us. Like the baby, however, we tend to think we have really accomplished something ourselves. When prayer becomes a joy and our faults disappear, we think it is a sign that we have really learned to walk in the ways of God. The reality is quite different: God is carrying us in his arms. Our faults (our inability to walk) have not been eliminated, but merely temporarily masked by God's grace. He, too, like the father of the baby, sets us down again—prayer becomes difficult and our failings return, and we find our whole situation very frustrating. Once we have known the joy of walking with the Lord, we can never again be satisfied with crawling on our bellies on the earth.

This is a critical and dangerous turning point in our

life of prayer. It is humiliating to realize that, left to ourselves, we are only good for crawling. We are tempted to feel that our experience of prayer must have been self-deception, that God has abandoned us, that prayer is a waste of time for us. None of this is true, of course, but the devil works overtime to convince us that we are failures. Sound spiritual direction and regular reading in the masters of prayer[6] are essential if we are to overcome the devil and our own wounded pride.

If we recall the goal of the life of prayer—the fruits of the Spirit grounded in a true knowledge of who God is and who I am—we can realize that what looks like failure is really growth. By carrying us in his arms for a time, the Lord has taught us that there is another world, far better than the crawler's world of man left to himself. By setting us down again, the Lord teaches us that this new world is not within our own power to reach. It is here that our father-baby analogy breaks down. The baby *will* gradually learn to walk for himself. The day will come when he is as tall as his father and can walk about the world on his own strong legs. But in the realm of prayer we are *always* babies, and we will always be carried on our Father's arms. The "little way" of the Little Flower, Therese of Lisieux, is ultimately the only way. This is precisely what she meant, that holiness is not the result of heroic efforts to improve ourselves but is the sheer gift of God's transforming love. Once we really learn this, the "dark night" will end and the Lord will lift us up to carry us forever.

How long will it take for us to learn this? John of the Cross, who calls the frustrating experience of our own helplessness and God's absence the "dark night of the senses," says that it is the lot of most faithful pray-ers for most of their lives. The Lord will pick us up from time to

---

[6]Boase's *Prayer of Faith,* Teresa's *Interior Castle* (Second and Third Mansions), John of the Cross's *Dark Night of the Soul* (Book I), and Merton's *Contemplative Prayer* are very helpful guides at this crucial stage of the interior life.

time. There will be occasional glimmers of light in the darkness, to reassure us and to strengthen us to persevere. But the principal proof of the genuineness of our prayer—the evidence that we are on the right track despite the darkness—will be the growth in us of the fruits of the Spirit. Do I find myself—today as compared, say, to a year or two years ago—more humble, more sensitive to the needs of others, with a deeper hunger for God and for his justice among men, gentler in dealing with human frailty? If I do, then my prayer is genuine and I am on the right track, for these are the fruits of the Spirit of God. This kind of growth can come only from him.

Given these signs, we can proceed peacefully in darkness and leave all else to the Lord. He alone knows how long the log of wood needs to be scorched and blackened before it is ready to become fire. He alone is the Lord. Teresa of Avila expresses it beautifully in the last of her "Exclamations of the Soul to God":

> Blessed are those whose names are written in the book of . . . life. But if thou are among them, my soul, why art thou sad and why dost thou trouble me? Hope in God, for even now I will confess to Him my sins and His mercies and of them all I will make a song of praise and will breathe perpetual sighs to my Savior and my God. It may be that a day will come when my glory shall sing to Him and my conscience shall be no more afflicted, when at last all sighs and fears shall cease. But meanwhile in silence and in hope shall my strength be. Rather would I live and die in the expectation and hope of eternal life than possess all created things and all the blessings which belong to them, since these must pass away. Forsake me not, Lord; since I hope in Thee, may my hope not be confounded; may I ever serve Thee; do with me what Thou wilt.[7]

[7]*Exclamations of the Soul to God,* XVII (vol. II, p. 420 in the Peers edition).

The experience is very different from what we expected when we began to learn to pray. But our God is a God of surprises. To encounter the Lord personally in love is to be captured by him—and to be carried in his arms.